THE BOOK OF

hopes+
dreams

FOR GIRLS AND YOUNG WOMEN

doctor

actress

tri...

writ...

dancer

Animator

arti...

THE BOOK OF

hopes+
dreams

FOR GIRLS AND YOUNG WOMEN

NOTABLE WOMEN SHARE THEIR EXPERIENCES AND WISDOM

Edited by
Christine Aulicino and
JoAnn Deak, Ph.D.

LAUREL SCHOOL
SHAKER HEIGHTS, OHIO

Printed in the United States of America
Book design by Epstein Design Partners Inc.
Cover art by Louisa Lowe (front) and Zoe Conley (back). Quote on this page by Kirby Foote. Art on previous spread by Natalie Okal.

LIBRARY OF CONGRESS CATALOG CARD NUMBER: 99-73709
ISBN 0-9664066-1-3

For information on ordering additional copies of this book, visit our website at www.laurelschool.com.

contents

preface

This book grew out of an experience I had many years ago while reading a published letter written by Jacqueline Kennedy Onassis. She wrote of her love of books and what they had meant to her life. I never forgot her powerful words and the clarity with which she expressed herself. She inspired an idea for a project that would become my own dream – the creation of a book, which would contain letters from some of the great living women of this century, to read and share with my own daughters who are students at Laurel School.

I was given the opportunity to make this dream a reality when, in 1995, Laurel began to plan for its 100th anniversary the following year. I proposed a Centennial Celebration project creating an archival book that could serve as both a legacy and as an inspiration for girls and women. The book would contain original letters from significant women who had made a difference in the 20th century.

A committee of parents, alumnae and staff was formed to create the book. Over the next two years, women from around the world were invited to submit letters articulating their own child-hood dreams and their hopes and dreams for girls and young women in the next century. We are honored to present their letters filled with humor, wisdom and the very real proof that dreams are indeed a stepping stone to greatness.

I am forever grateful to a very dedicated and visionary group of women who served on *The Book of Hopes and Dreams* committee. Their hard work and dedication are what kept this project alive and made it a reality. My thanks go to parents Sawsan AlHaddad, Laura Barnard, and Holly Brooks; Laurel School alumnae Gina Tippit Cronin, Myra Evans Lapeyrolerie, and Wendy Hoge Naylor; and staff members Wilhelmena Holmes, Julie Donahue and Alicia Reale. Special thanks to Wendy Naylor and Holly Brooks, in particular, for their exhaustive research, which was essential for reaching the contributors in this book. Thanks go as well to Anna Quindlen who served as Honorary Chair for the project. Last, but by no means least, my gratitude goes to Christine Aulicino and JoAnn Deak for their tenacity to push forward and publish.

CRICKETT KARSON

Chair, The Book of Hopes and Dreams *Committee*

Spring 1999

foreword

The book that you hold in your hands is truly a dream come true for Laurel School. The brain-child of Laurel Trustee and parent Crickett Karson, *The Book of Hopes and Dreams* began as a project of the school's Centennial year in 1996-97. Under the leadership of its creative and dynamic co-chairs, Laurel alumna Aloise O'Brien Bates and Laurel parent Sheila Wyse, the Centennial provided an appropriate moment to reach out to women around the world who are tremendous role models for the girls and young women who will succeed them. The statements compiled in this volume represent women with a remarkable range of backgrounds, interests, beliefs and professional choices. Yet, they share many of the ideals we at Laurel School seek to nurture in our students — curiosity, perseverance, a sense of connection to the larger world, a willingness to take risks, a respect for differences, and a passion for learning, in all of its richness and complexity. We hope that their words, along with the responses of Laurel School students, will inspire you to dream big dreams, to pursue them in ways that are satisfying, to make your own mark in our world and to make a difference. Each one of us has enormous potential. May this book help you to find and fulfill yours.

It is fitting that *The Book of Hopes and Dreams* has been the project of Laurel School. For more than 100 years, this school has been dedicated to giving girls and young women a first-rate education to prepare them for success in college and whatever subsequent paths they choose to pursue. Laurel provides a well-rounded curriculum encompassing a vast array of opportunities and challenges in academics, in athletics and in the arts. A deep commitment to community service engenders in students, from their youngest years, a connection to the larger world and a sense of the importance of volunteerism throughout their lives. Laurel School came to national prominence as the site of a five-year research study on girls' learning and decision-making styles led by Carol Gilligan and Lyn Mickel Brown of Harvard University. Their results were published in 1992 in *Meeting at the Crossroads: Women's Psychology and Girls' Development*, a work that is now part of the growing cannon of literature on girls' development. *The Book of Hopes and Dreams* is an important and meaningful extension of Laurel School's continued focus on identifying and addressing issues related to nurturing strong, independent and self-confident women.

Many fine minds and dedicated hands among Laurel School's faculty and staff have participated in realizing this wonderful project. Christine Aulicino brought renewed vitality to the project when it had lost momentum and encouraged us to see that this publication was not only possible, but important for Laurel to undertake for a national audience. We owe Christine a great debt of gratitude for her conviction and involvement in shaping the book. JoAnn Deak, our resident expert in the development of girls, played an invaluable role in broadening the scope of the book and bringing children's voices into the mix. Together Christine and JoAnn added a curricular component to the book and wrote introductory material and chapter prologues. A number of faculty members in each division were instrumental in integrating this project into their classroom curriculum. In the Primary Division, we are grateful to Kristen Anderson, Ellen Neebes, Pat Chapman and Ellen Mosier (Kindergarten); Joan Moody (First Grade); Jan Carr and Terri Garfinkel (Second Grade); Sarah Crissman and Signe Forbes (Third Grade); Rebecca Klar and Karen Sunderhaft (Fourth Grade); and Carin Truden. In the Middle School, we thank Eighth Grade English teacher Donna Caputo and Sixth Grade English teacher Ann Esselstyn. In the Upper School, we are grateful to history teacher Claudia Boatright. These dynamic teachers brought the project to life for their students and engaged them in vital ways in its creation. Special thanks are due to Gabriele Gossner, Laurel's Director of Development and External Affairs, for her vigilance in keeping the project moving forward and for raising the funds needed to make this book possible. Thanks also go to Julie Donahue and Colette Briere of our Communications Office, and Alicia Reale, formerly our Communications Assistant, for their efforts throughout the process. We thank Diana Tittle for her skillful editorial contributions and for her service as project manager. We thank Marla Gutzwiller and Gina Linehan of Epstein Design Partners Inc., whose sensitive design gives *The Book of Hopes and Dreams* its lively and elegant look.

We acknowledge, with deep gratitude for their generous support of this project, an alumna who wishes to remain anonymous, the McNerny family — Jim, Haity, Julia, Hilary and Robert — whose gift was made in honor of JoAnn Deak, and the Cleveland City Women's Club Foundation.

My wish for girls and women everywhere is that this book will resonate with you in powerful, enduring ways. Happy reading!

HELEN ROWLAND
MARTER

Head of School
Spring 1999

introduction

"My hopes and dreams for girls around the world are simple,"

writes First Lady Hillary Rodham Clinton.

"I hope that every girl can grow up to fulfill her own dreams

and ambitions in a world at peace."

Too bad that "wishing doesn't make it so," as our mothers used to tell us. Despite the gains of the women's movement, the world still bases pay unequally on gender and imposes a "glass ceiling" on females in almost every field of endeavor. Worse yet, it places the self-esteem and confidence of girls and young women at risk by valuing beauty over brains and character.

What does seem to have a significant, positive effect on the development of females? In the last ten years, girls and young women have been studied and written about more than ever before, and there is mounting evidence that several factors can influence favorably their growth and development. One of the most important factors is the presence in their lives of strong and diverse female role models.

Recognizing that the majority of girls will never have the opportunity to meet and interact with the most accomplished women of our day, Laurel School has decided to publish a collection of inspirational letters written to its students by notable women from around the world and from many different walks of life. *The Book of Hopes and Dreams*, a compilation of excerpts from these heartfelt letters, accompanied by biographical information about their authors, will give successive generations of females the opportunity to draw guidance and encouragement from the wisdom of women who have achieved great success in the arts, athletics, government, law, medicine, scientific research, political action, journalism, publishing, business, education and religious life. Just as the faculty, administration and parents of Laurel School have enjoyed sharing and discussing with our students the life stories and positive messages contained in these letters, we hope that mothers and grandmothers, teachers and mentors, aunts and godmothers will use *The Book of Hopes and Dreams* to demonstrate to the girls and young women they love that women can achieve any goal to which they commit their hearts and minds.

Indeed, this is the good news underpinning each of the letters, which have been edited for clarity and brevity and otherwise remain as written. Many of the authors also convey their hopeful visions of the future. What do they wish for our daughters and granddaughters? The same things we want for our sons and grandsons: opportunities for self-fulfillment and the chance to live an ethical and caring life in a world that is safe and healthy.

While the women's voices are wonderfully singular, we detected some recurring motifs in their messages, prompting our decision to group the letters into thematic chapters. We also decided to interweave the responses of some of Laurel's students, who were asked to reflect on this unique collection of letters as part of their classwork. When invited to express their hopes for their own futures, our students responded enthusiastically: in poetry and prose, in dreams for themselves and in wishes for younger girls, in sketches, drawings and computer-generated art. Like girls everywhere, they dream of becoming astronauts, doctors, dancers, gymnasts, professional athletes, artists, mothers, wives, veterinarians, architects and political leaders. They want to abolish poverty and war, save the environment and find a cure for cancer. Their voices are strong, confident and idealistic, underscoring the validity of research that has demonstrated the importance of single-gender experiences in promoting self-esteem in girls.

There was a compelling reason for encouraging the girls at Laurel to contribute to *The Book of Hopes and Dreams*. Research has identified an important factor that has a positive influence on the development of females: doing. Females who accomplish things, who participate in interactive learning experiences, who take risks, who perform, tend to develop stronger self-esteem. That is, they are more confident and competent, more willing and able to interact successfully with and in the world. By asking our girls to engage in a "dialogue" with the adult letter writers, we accomplished several objectives simultaneously: we exposed our students to strong female voices and role models; boosted their self-esteem by demonstrating respect for their "voices;" and provided a meaningful experience of "doing," i.e., writing for possible publication. At the same time, we hoped to enhance the value of *The Book of Hopes and Dreams* in the eyes of its intended young audience by providing musings and material to which girls and young women could relate directly.

Laurel's faculty members chose a variety of pedagogical approaches to prompt their students to think about their hopes and dreams for the future.

In Kindergarten, our computer teacher read aloud selections of the letters to the girls. The students then went to their computers and drew pictures of their own aspirations.

Our Second Graders read and studied forms of poetry as part of their curriculum. After their homeroom teachers read a selection of letters to them, they responded in verse.

The Third Graders read and had read to them one of the chapters in this book. They then composed narratives describing their own hopes and dreams.

Fourth-Grade teachers asked their students to imagine themselves as all grown up and to write a letter to their Fourth-Grade selves from that vantage point.

Sixth Graders spent their English classes discussing the letters and then envisioned their futures.

Eighth Graders read selected letters, discussed their reactions to the inspiration found in the letters, and wrote reflections about their own dreams and aspirations.

Seniors wrote letters to the youngest members of the Laurel community, the Preschoolers. Their letters poignantly share their wishes for the little ones.

Taken as a whole, the prose, poetry and pictures produced by our students, who range in age from five to eighteen, certainly reflect what we know about developmental stages of females. Kindergarteners drew joyous pictures of their fantasies or portrayed themselves as following in the footsteps of a beloved adult. Primary girls and beginning Middle Schoolers tended to be more specific about their aspirations, e.g., wanting to be a veterinarian or an artist. Developmentally, this cohort is quite literal in its interpretation of the world, and girls of this age seek to fit themselves into established categories.

By late Middle School, the classic "shoulds" started to appear in our students' work. This is the age at which young women want the world to be more of an ideal place. Thus, girls should do what they love, women should be able to do anything. The oldest students, the Seniors, revealed their budding adulthood by taking their assignment very seriously. They tried to bring all of their hard-earned wisdom to bear in their advice for the next generation.

This book represents the accumulated wisdom of a cross-generational discussion we at Laurel School are proud to have initiated: notable women forthrightly sharing their life experiences and insights with a younger generation of females, and girls and young women responding to their mentors with expressions of their innermost wishes for their own lives. As Ambassador Pamela Harriman wrote to us before her untimely death: "We must do everything in our power to encourage girls to believe in themselves, believe in each other, and seek, as individuals and members of the larger community, the fulfillment of their dreams." May *The Book of Hopes and Dreams* play a small part in that critical endeavor.

JoAnn Deak, Ph.D.
Director of the
Primary Division

Christine Aulicino
Director of the
Middle School

Spring 1999

dream **big** glorious powerful

Chapter One

When I

grow up,

I want

to be a

famous

artist.

Susannah Conway
KINDERGARTEN

dreams

Dreams are the very stuff of childhood.

In the letters featured in this chapter, the authors speak of their own

dreams and how they were encouraged or discouraged from follow-

ing them. How many women growing up a generation ago did not pur-

sue the careers of their dreams because certain fields were closed to them?

Many of the letter writers achieved recognition because they refused to give

up, and their advice to girls of today is to hold on to dreams in the face of all odds.

In urging young women to "dream big, glorious, powerful dreams," Judge Patricia Ann

Blackmon writes that, although she grew up in circumstances that many might describe as

difficult, her dreams led her to believe that "every aspect of [her] life was laced with possibilities."

1

I was always fascinated by animals. When I was four years old we stayed on a farm where I helped to collect hens' eggs — no cruel battery farms then. It seems I became puzzled, asking "Where is the hole big enough for the eggs to come out?" When no one answered to my satisfaction I hid in a small stuffy hen-house for some four hours to find out. And when my mother finally saw me rushing towards the house, she noticed my excitement and instead of scolding me (the family had even called the police!) she sat down to hear the wonderful story of how a hen lays an egg.

My first books were about animals. *Dr. Doolittle* and *Tarzan*. By the time I was eight years old I knew what I wanted to do when I grew up; go to Africa, live with animals, and write books about them. But in those days young people — especially girls — did not go tramping off into the jungle. Moreover, Africa was still "The Dark Continent" and very far away. And although we always had plenty to eat, we didn't have enough money for luxuries — we didn't have a car and couldn't afford a bicycle. But I talked about going to Africa all the time. And my mother — a very special person — used to say "Jane, if you really want something, and if you work hard, and take advantage of opportunities, and never give up, you will somehow find a way."

To get a grant for university [study] in those days was difficult; you had to be good in a foreign language and I was hopeless. So when I left school I did a secretarial course — so that I would be able to get work anywhere in the world. I got a wonderful job with a documentary film company — but I went on dreaming and reading books about African animals. Then came a letter inviting me to stay with a friend in Kenya. How could I get the fare? My job paid very little, and I'd saved almost nothing. I went home and worked as a waitress, saving up my wages and tips until I had enough for a return fare to Kenya by boat — the cheapest way then.

Later I heard about Louis Leakey and went to see him. Because I knew so much about African animals, he gave me a job at the natural history museum in Nairobi. Then I went with Louis and his wife, Mary, on their summer fossil-hunting expedition to the now-famous Olduvai Gorge. It wasn't famous then, in 1957 — no prehistoric human remains had yet been discovered. It was wild, and there were so many animals. Every evening, after the hard day's work, I walked on the plains. Once I met a black rhino. Another time a couple of two-year-old male lions. I wonder if you can imagine what it was like? I'd dreamed of Africa all my life and I was actually living in my dream!

Louis decided I was the person he'd been looking for to go to a game reserve on the shores of Lake Tanganyika to try to find out about chimpanzee behaviour. It was hard for him to get funding – I had no degree, no formal training – but eventually he got some seed money from a wealthy American businessman – and I could start.

I have told my story because it shows anything is possible if you heed my mother's advice – which I now share with you. Follow your dream. Don't let anyone tell you it is impossible; work hard, take advantage of opportunity, and NEVER GIVE UP. Remember, what you do, as an individual, makes a difference. You cannot live through a day without impacting the world around you. And you have a choice – do you want to make the world a better place – for the environment, animals and people? Or don't you care?

JANE GOODALL, PH.D.
Wildlife researcher and conservationist

I always wanted to become a doctor, ever since I was a child. I remember my first inexpensive medical box that my grandmother gave me for my third birthday. I've had my dream of becoming a doctor for a very long time and I hope I never lose it.

I think what made me interested in medicine was after I heard my mother's story about coming to America, not knowing English that well, and how she went to medical school here. Every one of you reading this could go into medicine. It's not the blood and gore of it all I'm after. Everyone could get used to that. It's the knowledge that you are not going to give up your dream, and I have a feeling I will never do that.

DANA ATAYA
SIXTH GRADE

When I was growing up, I dreamed of becoming a filmmaker. But in those days, it seemed an impossible dream – to everyone but me, at least. There really were no women filmmakers. And there was no such thing as a film school where I (or anyone else!) could learn how to become one. As far as my family and friends were concerned, I might as well have said I dreamed of going to Mars; that's how far-fetched my dream appeared to them. Thus, on top of having to nourish and pursue a difficult dream, I had the added burden of hiding my dream from others, and a total lack of support and encouragement from everyone important to me.

And so, when I dream of an ideal future for the girls of today, I look to a time when every girl will be able to imagine herself in any role she dreams of, when no one will discourage her from pursuing that dream, and when our society will offer her every chance to succeed in making her dream come true. I dream that a girl will aspire to be President of the United States, and then win that office, voted in by millions of Americans confident in her ability to lead them.

If such dreams are to come to reality, our country must mature and grow in many ways – and I hope it does.

I hope that our country will be a place of peace, prosperity and compassion so that no girls go in want of food, shelter, clothing, medical care and – most important of all – love.

I hope that our society will provide all girls with a full range of opportunities; and that no aspiration is disparaged or forbidden on the basis of their gender.

I hope that all girls will have access to a quality education, which will teach them the skills they need to move toward their dreams, and prepare them to manage successfully each responsibility they undertake on their way to the top.

I hope that every girl will enjoy the self-respect that comes with self-knowledge and ability. I hope that she will respect others as she respects herself, and that others will accord her the same honor and dignity.

I hope that every girl pauses to appreciate each step on the road to her dream, that she feels joy in the process of learning, and a passion for the life she has chosen, for it is from this that success is born and achieves its full worth.

Lastly, I hope that each girl remembers to share her good fortune with others; and that she uses her success to good purpose by taking the time and effort to help others achieve their dreams.

SHERRY LANSING
Chairman, Paramount Studios

If you want to do your greatest dream,

you've got to shout it out

so everyone can hear you.

You've got to keep trying

and do it your hardest.

You've got to dream

your dream

every night.

And when you've done it,

you've got to shine like a star

and say "I did that."

LINDA KATIRJI

THIRD GRADE

As a girl I wanted to be Nancy Drew, because she was the only out-of-the-home successful modern woman I had read about. Now, thank goodness, young women have more choices. We owe many of today's expanded opportunities to women who were not afraid to dream big dreams and to act on them. I hope that today's girls will feel free to stretch their options further, to dream still bigger dreams, to pursue them with confidence, and to be proud of their accomplishments.

But in expanding the limits of their own achievements, I hope that today's girls will think of the welfare of others. I hope that they will remember that just as girls have enjoyed fewer opportunities than boys, so many people today face enormous disadvantages — lack of education, poor health, poverty. So I hope that today's girls will remember to make room for all people, girls and boys, men and women, in their dreams for the future. And I hope that when today's girls grow into successful women, they will feel an obligation to help the next generation of young women.

NINA TOTENBERG
Correspondent and commentator, National Public Radio

I have been through many of what I consider "phases," which I call, "When I grow up, I want to be. . . ." In these phases, I have wanted to become more things than anyone without a HUGE imagination could ever think of! I have wanted to be: an astronaut, a teacher, a princess, a dragon, a pilot, a psychologist, and more! These "I want to be when I grow ups" never lasted long. But for three years now, I have wanted to be a doctor — a pediatric surgeon.

MORGAN RAYE
SIGMAN
SIXTH GRADE

In the suburban town where I grew up all the schools were named after famous writers. I attended Nathaniel Hawthorne Public School for the early grades, and, later, Ralph Waldo Emerson. The portraits of these two distinguished figures were displayed in the school entrance halls: bearded gentlemen wearing frock coats and cravats, immensely dignified and serious in their expressions. They were writers; they were men; they were dead. Clearly they belonged to a privileged world from which I was excluded.

Nevertheless, I decided to become a writer. The resolution formed very early in my life, but it took years for me to discover what I would write about and who my readers would be.

Several layers of trust were required before I began to find my direction. I had to learn to rely on my own voice, and after that to have faith in the value of my own experiences. At first this was frightening. The books I read as a child related daring adventures, deeds of courage. The stories took place on mountaintops or in vast cities, not in the sort of quiet, green suburb where my family happened to live. It was as though there was an empty space on the bookshelf. No one seemed to talk about this void, yet I knew it was there.

Gradually I understood that the books I should write were the very books I wanted to read, the books I wasn't able to find in the library. The empty place could be closed. My small world might fill only a page at first, then several hundred pages, possibly thousands. I could make up in accuracy for what I lacked in scope, getting the details right, dividing every experience into its various shades and levels of anticipation. I could write a story, for instance, about Nathaniel Hawthorne School. About the school principal whose name was Miss Newbury (Miss Blueberry she was called behind her back). About the chill of fear children suffered in the schoolyard, about a fat, suffering little boy named Walter who had an English accent and whose mother made him wear a necktie to school. About human foolishness, and about the small rescues and acts of redemption experienced along the way.

I saw that I could become a writer if I paid attention, if I was careful, if I observed the rules, and then, just as carefully, broke them.

CAROL SHIELDS
Pulitzer Prize-winning author and educator

SKATING

If I could have my dream,

I'd make the Olympic team,

To be the world's best figure skater,

Nothing could be greater.

Axels, toe-loops, spins and such,

Do the waltz that I think is Dutch,

Nothing could be greater,

Eleanor Anderson,

champion figure skater!

ELEANOR ANDERSON
THIRD GRADE

My hopes and dreams are that I can always remain hopeful and dreaming. Furthermore, that hopefulness and dreaming aren't limited to the young, the privileged or the naive. I hope that the richness of being alive can become so much more textured by our ability to create great art and a civilization's legacy. My hope and dream is to be knowing, observant and (I hope) funny.

WENDY WASSERSTEIN

Pulitzer Prize-winning playwright

I grew up in Jackson, Mississippi, during the civil rights era. Our community was extremely poor. My mother worked several jobs to feed and clothe us. I spent many days dreaming about my future, planning my world, and setting forth my goals. I knew early on that I wanted to be a lawyer and that I would do great and wonderful things. My dreams and my hopes sustained me and made me who I am today. Every aspect of my life was laced with possibilities. So, I urge you to dream big, glorious, powerful dreams.

I wish you a world laced with opportunities and possibilities. I hope that you will see obstacles in your path as bumps in the road; bumps that you can move over and around with ease, if you try.

I wish for you the ability to try, to take risks, and to negotiate opportunities. My mother often told me that failure is always defeated when one tries.

And, above all, I hope that when you are older, you will make the world better for all girls to live in; that you will take the world beyond racism, hatred, and bias; that you will become the leaders of this world; that your sons and daughters will be nurtured and cared for as you were; and that you succeed at every moment.

I wish for you peace in your soul and also to know that you are here on earth for a reason and it is by divine order. I hope you believe that the universe is conspiring to give you everything that you want. I hope that you ride the wave of every opportunity and have an open heart to every possibility; for impossible things are happening every day.

PATRICIA ANN BLACKMON

Administrative Judge, Court of Appeals of Ohio

DREAMING

Swish,
Swish
through
my
head,
over
the
rainbow
in
my
bed,
there
will
be
no
bad
thoughts
because
I
can
dream
anything
I
want.

CHRISTY CARDELLINI
THIRD GRADE

Chapter Two

I want

to work

with jewels.

Katharine Mintz
KINDERGARTEN

imagine freely

The dreams of children are sorted and sifted over time, leading the dreamer to choices.

Every child has made the choice to either stick with an inspiring plan or

to abandon an outgrown dream. In this chapter, the contributors encourage

girls to make their own choices and not to allow others to dictate their life

decisions. "Imagine freely," and "feel no limits" urges novelist Joyce Carol Oates.

Women such as Eleanor Clift and Donna Ferrato, whose letters you will read in this

chapter, recall how they shaped their futures by making important choices. Sometimes

choices arise from serendipitous circumstances; sometimes choices are made on "gut instinct."

Yet all of these accomplished women acknowledge that choosing among dreams is crucial.

My hopes and dreams for girls around the world are simple. I hope that every girl can grow up to fulfill her own dreams and ambitions in a world at peace.

More than thirty years ago, I wrote a letter to NASA about my dreams of becoming an astronaut, only to get a letter back saying that women weren't allowed in the space program. Today, four years shy of the 21st century and a new millennium, the sky literally doesn't have to be the limit for American girls. Girls can realistically dream of flying in space (as I write this essay, one American woman scientist is living and working in a space station), piloting jet fighters, and running Fortune 500 companies. They can be Supreme Court justices, network television anchors, and big-city police chiefs. They can choose full-time motherhood and homemaking.

I hope every girl will understand that there is no set formula for how she should lead her life. Each of us must be free to make the most of our interests, talents, and desires. But with this abundance of choice comes responsibility – a responsibility to respect the decisions other women make for themselves and their families, as well as the responsibility to use our gifts to serve our communities. In a world where so many children are still growing up unfed, unhealthy, and unschooled, I hope all girls and boys and men and women will work to extend opportunities to others whose life choices are limited by social, political, cultural, and economic constraints.

HILLARY RODHAM CLINTON
First Lady

When I was about five years old, I wanted to be whatever my parents were. So I asked them what their professions were and they told me. Then I said I was going to have that profession. My mother then said, "Abby, you should be whatever you feel like being." The next day I started thinking about my profession.

I have come upon the decision to be a vet, and to write about my experiences, like James Herriot. I do not want to be exactly like him, because I want to be an individual, but I feel that I desire to follow in his footsteps.

ABIGAIL MURPHY
SIXTH GRADE

Hopes and dreams! — there's an aura of solemnity here that, while certainly appropriate, shouldn't be misleading. To be a "girl" — to be a "woman" — to be "female" — need not be presented as a solemn enterprise entirely, or exclusively. Girls can grow up to be competitive with men; we former girls have turned out quite well, over the decades — we're surgeons, doctors, medical researchers; lawyers, executives, film and TV producers, directors, and performers; we're athletes, astronauts, anthropologists, astrophysicists, teachers, university professors, photographers, artists, writers, world explorers. We seem to have transcended a historical epoch in which "biology is fate" was the ground rule, and sexual identity was automatically personal identity.

My dream for a girl of our time is that she can imagine freely, and feel no limits constraining her. She can exult in being a "girl" — which is a condition to be enjoyed — and she can exult in being an individual, undefined by gender. If love, friendship, nurturing and a sense of family responsibility have been qualities traditionally associated with women, she can take pride in this fact, but consider, too, that a woman is an individual, in essence.

JOYCE CAROL OATES
Novelist

When I was thirteen years old, I won an essay contest on the theme, "What the United Nations Means to Me." Eleanor Roosevelt, the widow of President Franklin Roosevelt, presented me with a $50 check and commented on the fact that we were both Eleanors. Even my last name was similar, she noted. (I was Eleanor Roeloffs then.) To be honored by such a great woman was thrilling for me. I wish I could say that from that moment on, I wanted to be a journalist. But the truth is that I never thought, even as a young girl, that such a glorious profession could be accessible to me. During the '50s and early '60s, when I came of age, the gender stereotyping of women limited my aspirations to a handful of occupations. Nursing, teaching, and office work were the areas women were expected to choose. I started working at *Newsweek* as a secretary because I wanted to work where what I typed would be interesting.

During the '60s, the great social movements of civil rights and women's liberation stirred the country's conscience. The women at *Newsweek* filed a lawsuit against the magazine charging discrimination. *Newsweek* responded by creating internships for women, and by agreeing to a court-ordered affirmative action plan to place women in reporting and writing positions. Although I had never taken a journalism course and did not have a college degree, I believed I could do the job. I applied for an internship and, almost ten years after joining *Newsweek* as a secretary, I became a reporter. Not long after that, I was assigned to cover the presidential campaign of Jimmy Carter, a candidate my editors thought was going nowhere. When Carter won the election, I went with him to Washington as *Newsweek's* White House reporter.

I tell this Cinderella story to make the point that most of us get where we are by serendipity, if we put ourselves in position to take advantage of good fortune when it comes our way. Young girls today have almost boundless opportunities in the world, yet it is often life's seeming accidents, a burst of fortune or even misfortune, that determines the path a person takes. Listen to your heart and don't abandon your dreams. That's how you win in the long run.

Early in his term, President Jimmy Carter summoned me to the Oval Office to talk about a controversial trip to Latin America that First Lady Rosalynn Carter was about to undertake. A substantial portion of the electorate thought Mrs. Carter was overstepping her role. The President referred to his wife as "my Eleanor." I knew exactly what he meant. Eleanor Roosevelt's name has come to symbolize both independence and humanitarian concern. She lived her life, for herself and for others, in enviable balance.

My hope for girls today is that they have the courage to do what they think is right, and that they find balance in their lives between work and family in an increasingly competitive and complex world. I recently attended a friend's fiftieth birthday party. His daughter thanked her parents for teaching their children to be "thinkers, doers and believers." By developing these skills, you can dream your own dreams and see them come true.

ELEANOR CLIFT
Contributing editor, Newsweek

THE ROAD THAT LIES AHEAD

When I was little, I decided to become a pediatric neurologist, but I've given up that idea now. I'd like to teach something in college. That would be interesting, and I'd like to be a teacher. But I'd also like to become a doctor, or do something with computers. And perhaps I could also write, in my spare time, and maybe write a world- famous book. Of course, I'll never give up reading. If there was a job where all you had to do was read, well, then I'd definitely know which job to take!

NILOUFER KHAN
SIXTH GRADE

When

I am

older

I want

to be

a famous

singer,

a famous

skater, and

a famous

Beanie Baby

collector.

JENNIFER HARDING
THIRD GRADE

I am highly optimistic about the world of opportunities that girls like my daughter will have when they choose their paths in life. We have seen women become astronauts, senators, governors, fighter pilots, poet laureates, and Supreme Court justices; and we've even seen a woman become chief executive officer of a major global ad agency. Now that women have arrived at the point where, having proved beyond a shadow of a doubt that we can do everything, we've at last won (better yet, earned) the freedom to do what we want. My deepest desire is for every girl to follow her dreams and grow up to live her life doing whatever she wants to do.

ROCHELLE (SHELLY) B. LAZARUS
Chairman and chief executive officer,
Ogilvy & Mather Worldwide

When I grow up I want to be the first woman President in the world. And if I don't win, I'll be a famous figure skater. Or I'll do gymnastics for fun. But my biggest dream is to be the first woman President.

ALEXANDRA
KENNEDY
SECOND GRADE

Most people find that life is full of choices. There is no single path to follow. My own career path was haphazard. I had no game plan. Instead, I pursued areas that truly interested me. I would encourage you to do the same. Because if you love what you do, that's where you will find satisfaction. If you want to be at home and raise children, that's great. If you want to be a rocket scientist or corporate executive, do it. Or if you feel good about a career that is not "high-power" but you find fulfilling, that's fine. You can spend your life trying to please friends, spouses, bosses and parents, but unless you can look in the mirror and say "I like who I am and what I have become," you won't be happy.

FARAH M. WALTERS
President and chief executive officer,
University Hospitals of Cleveland

I wrote about my hopes and dreams in fourth grade and I think if I looked at it today I would think, MAN, WHAT THE HECK WAS I THINKING? People change, you get bored with things, you get interested in new things, you change. Here is my list of hopes and dreams for SIXTH GRADE!!! I have become interested in tennis. My tennis coach, Hari, really makes tennis a lot of fun. When I grow up I want to be either a very important, famous, or pro tennis player. I also might want to be a tennis teacher.

I bet in at least two years this list will change a lot.

CHRISTINA LANZIERI
SIXTH GRADE

The woman I am today grew out of the unrepentant "girl power" that flowed in the blood of Laurel's rebel class of 1968. We had within us a dangerous combination of desire, despair, and disillusionment. On graduation day, our headmaster's speech fell flat because our ears were still ringing from the gunshots which destroyed our hope for the future. Bobby Kennedy killed, like Martin Luther King Jr., within weeks of each other.

I've spent years trying to capture the deadly effects of violence often committed in the name of love. The way I live reflects a need to see what makes sense, to fill my life with people and things which bring joy. Photography, which is how I make a living, gives me passion to try to change things. The camera has been my constant companion for more than two decades.

As a photographer, I've witnessed what happens when women relinquish control over their world. I've seen how it happens when women in love convince themselves a sacrifice is necessary – abandoning their dignity, their desires, their dreams. What happens when women choose to stand by untrustworthy, abusive mates is that they harm and degrade not only themselves but their children and grandchildren.

As the mother of a fiercely proud teenager, I have the same dream day in, day out. I'm hoping Fanella will learn to listen to her gut instincts; believe in her own bold voice. I'm praying she will grab hold of that wondrous fire in her young body and never let it go. I'm wanting the intimacy she will undoubtedly crave with others ultimately to set her free.

These and four more are my wishes for today's girls: first, that they be aware of their limitless potential; second, that they be smart in their search for love, knowing that jealousy and possession have nothing to do with love; third, that they remove the word "victim" from their vocabulary; fourth, that they know they'll still be fine, even if there's not always a man around.

DONNA FERRATO
Photojournalist and Laurel School Distinguished Alumna

People told me that I was never

going to be an actress. But when

it came to my parents, they

knew I would. In came my

sisters, and they thought

I would have stage fright.

So I'm trying to ignore

them. And I'm working

my way to be the best.

The best the world has

ever seen. The Best!! But

then again, I'm still young.

ALEXANDRA FOX
THIRD GRADE

Chapter Three

I love

to jump

rope.

Rebecca Barnard
KINDERGARTEN

do what you love

A passion for the work and life a girl chooses is seen as an essential ingredient for success. "Love what you do and do what you love" is the wisdom shared by the women whose letters are featured here. Diane Sawyer remembers being so advised by her father; Suzanne Farrell heard similar advice from her mentor, George Balanchine. The fourth-grade voice of Jillian describes the joy of exhaustion she feels after "playing her heart out" on the drums. It becomes clear when reading the letters throughout this chapter that a love for, a passion for, one's dream can make the dream a reality and lead the dreamer to find a meaningful way to contribute to the community.

Over the years we have heard dancers tell us how painful it is to dance, how much they had to give up, how difficult life was, and what sacrifices were demanded of them to be able to be successful in their chosen profession. Let me emphasize that I don't feel that way at all. I made a completely voluntary commitment to ballet very early in my life, probably at about twelve years old. Most ballet dancers have to do this…otherwise we cannot go through the preparation and adopt the discipline of body, mind, and emotions that are necessary to give us the physical and moral strength to dance.

Up there on that stage we may look as if we are floating on air; our fast steps and turns, our jumps and pirouettes may look magically easy. Of course, that is all an illusion. A good dancer needs the body of an athlete and the mind and spirit of an artist. The work we do, the endless hours of class and rehearsal are not supposed to show. If they do, performance is not successful. Dancing requires incredible concentration. We can't look at the audience to see its reaction. We have to focus entirely on what we are doing in the split second in which we do it. And we have to do it full out: the best we can. We cannot, and should not, say to ourselves: "Today I'll

SUZANNE FARRELL
Ballet dancer

do it halfway; tomorrow I'll do it better." For a dancer, that just doesn't work. The time span of our career is just too short. Indeed, life is too short.

Out of this concentration on the moment, on the awareness of that moment as it actually is and what it holds, comes what I consider the most important part of my philosophy. My most profound commitment is to the "now" of life. I feel that I must experience and use every moment as I live it, because I will never have that particular moment again.

George Balanchine, the great choreographer, was also a great influence on my life and on my ideas. When he taught ballet class, he would often say to us: "Why are you holding back? What are you waiting for? Do it now!" I translated this advice into the way I tried to live my life.

Out of this strict discipline came great freedom and serenity. I acquired a commitment to excellence for its own sake — and the joy that such a commitment can bring along with all the hard work. Often I danced 12 hours a day — and there was absolutely nothing that I would rather have done. As a result, I am a happy person. I do not brood because it makes the moment you are living in unavailable to learning, understanding and to joy.

Being
absolutely,
passionately
devoted
to work
and my
profession
makes me
feel lucky
indeed.
I feel
fortunate
that
I can have
a career
that is so
fulfilling,
and hope
that all
of you
will too.

JULIA CHILD
*Gourmet chef
and author*

I don't know what I want to be when I grow up, but I know that I want to be an athlete in a sport that I love, and I want to work at a job that I love.

Some people want to be famous and have more money than the richest person in the world. Money or fame is not important to me. As long as I have my family and do what I love for a living, I will be the happiest person in the world.

MANDY KOVACH
SIXTH GRADE

I'll always remember my father's simple but galvanizing questions when I graduated from college and couldn't find the right road to begin the journey. "What do you love doing?" he asked. "Writing," I answered. "So, where is the most adventurous place to do what you love, be challenged?" And I was on my way.

DIANE SAWYER
Broadcast journalist, ABC News

What I want to be when I grow up is one of the best female drummers. Since in my basement I have a drum set, everyday I walk downstairs and sit down and play my little heart out. Everyday since I got these drums I've wanted to make up a new song or tune. What I love most is when I spin the mallets in my hands. Most of the time my hands hurt while I'm walking up the stairs. Sometimes I can't even hold my fork. Nothing in the world is more interesting than the drums!

JILLIAN CASSIDY
FOURTH GRADE

MY DREAM

I had a dream since I was a little girl.
It was to be a famous singer.
I loved to sing. Once I found a
wishing well. I made a wish that
I could be a famous singer at
age eight. I was going to be
eight in three days. I was
wishing with all my heart.
I never wanted to change
my dream. I always will
want to be a singer and
if I keep on wishing it
just may come true.

ANA RELJANOVIC
SECOND GRADE

My hopes and dreams for girls are that they will be able to achieve their maximum potential doing work they love. The day when that should be possible has arrived, and each girl should take advantage of that possibility.

I think it is important for each girl to have a vision, a goal toward which she can aim her life. In my case it was a desire to be a scientist and to find a cure for cancer. I have made some contribution toward that goal, although I did not achieve as much as I would have liked. The pursuit of that goal made me persevere even when women were not welcomed as chemists in research laboratories. I hope I played a part in changing that attitude and making it easier for the young women who came after me.

Girls should pursue their dreams with confidence and determination. When they do, work becomes fun and achievement becomes a reality.

GERTRUDE B. ELION
Medical scientist and Nobel Laureate

Dear Amanda,

I hope you still want to play basketball in the W.N.B.A in ten years. I hope you want to travel to different countries and entertain the world. I hope you will always represent Puerto Rico, proud and strong. Remember, basketball is your life! Never give up on it.

AMANDA GOMEZ
FOURTH GRADE

Chapter Four

Don't
be afraid
to
climb
mountains.

Alyssa Hoffman
SECOND GRADE

take risks
make mistakes

Girls and risk-taking: it's a combination that many experts on child development claim they don't observe often. What really happens when a dream brings a girl or young woman face to face with risks, with the possibility of failure? One Third Grader states confidently that taking risks "can lead to success and happiness." By Eighth Grade, we hear the confession of a young adolescent who admits to "passing up great opportunities." The outstanding women whose letters are included in this chapter have faced risks, survived failures and gained a deeper understanding of themselves through their mistakes. They urge girls to find the strength to risk disappointment. Martina Navratilova states, "The only true failure is the failure to try."

Every experience we
have can be a source of
growth and blessing.
Even our mistakes can
teach us something.
I hope the girls of today
and tomorrow will
never be afraid to fail.
Success is sweet, but
when we have done our
best, we need not be
ashamed of failing.
Failure means that we
were not afraid to try.
Never forget that the
world moves forward
every day because
someone is willing to
take the risk. You can
be that someone.

SALLY J. PRIESAND
Rabbi

I hope you girls will use all the
possibilities open to you now,
take risks, make mistakes,
continue to evolve and grow,
and commit yourselves.

And in the end, you will use
everything, though perhaps
in unexpected ways.

BETTY FRIEDAN
Women's rights activist and author

To the Class of 2011:

Don't be afraid to use your voice;
don't be afraid to scream.
Make waves, state your opinion,
use strength and intelligence as
your weapons. Accept nothing
less than success. Take risks,
question authority, question
the answers.

ANGELA YOUNG
TWELFTH GRADE

DON'T GIVE UP

Climb,

Jump,

Work hard,

Don't give up.

Do not

let go of

your

lifelong

Dreams.

Break a leg

to reach

the top

of your

DREAMS.

Lauren Berger
Third Grade

Puzzles, I find, can be compared to your life. There are thousands of pieces scattered everywhere in all shapes and sizes. Through time, patience, and lots of intricate thought, the pieces slowly fit together to create a beautiful masterpiece. Right before you put the last piece in, you realize how far you have come. You see that without each and every piece, the puzzle wouldn't be a whole. Use this image to remember that every small piece of your life influences tomorrow, and to continue with confidence in yourself always.

MAYA ALBANESE
EIGHTH GRADE

Think of life as a series of course corrections. You don't get a map with detailed directions for your life, but you can set your own destination. Adjust your course as needed, but never forget your goal or ideal. I didn't know as a younger woman what my causes would be or where they would lead; I don't think you can know that yet. But you can consciously develop your personal assets and be open to ways of having an impact. Set off in a general direction or toward a thought of what you'd like to be or do; then "course correct" as you fine-tune what you like and don't like and how you want to have an impact at a particular time.

SARAH WEDDINGTON
Plaintiff's attorney, Roe v. Wade

I hope you find the courage to dream. And dream big. Don't be afraid of pushing your limits. And when you do find your limits, that's O.K. We are all different and sooner or later we all fail. The only true failure is the failure to try.

So my hope for you is this: Set your goal, give it your best (only you know if you are doing just that) and most of all — Enjoy yourself!

MARTINA
NAVRATILOVA

*Tennis legend and
Wimbledon champion*

If young women want to have a successful life this is my recipe: learn from your mistakes. If you don't, your mistakes will happen over and over again. Another step is to be bold and courageous. If you aren't, you will be pushed around and not listened to. Take a risk in life to make life interesting and challenging.

BETHA BOWEN
THIRD GRADE

MY DREAM

I wish I could go to the
Olympics and do a
cartwheel on the
balance beam,
do a no-handed
cartwheel, do a
headstand for two
minutes or more,
do a handstand
thirty-four seconds or
more, do the splits for
one minute or more,
do cool stuff on
the bars and win
a gold medal.

HANNAH ELLIOT
SECOND GRADE

> Do not be
> afraid to
> take risks.
> Do not be
> afraid to
> make mistakes.
> Any mistake
> you make paves
> the way for
> greater
> understanding
> and challenges.
>
> MURIEL SIEBERT
> *President
> and chairman,
> Muriel Siebert
> and Company*

You can't go through life not taking risks. Risks help you learn things. Risks can lead to success and happiness. Even if you aren't successful, you can get happiness out of knowing you tried your hardest. Take risks and the whole world will become your answer to all the questions you could ever ask.

AMANDA ORR
THIRD GRADE

I caught myself on occasion passing up great opportunities, quieting myself when I had something important to say, and being a complete sitting duck. I hesitated to do what I longed to do because I was afraid of what others would say or think. Take a chance! I guarantee that no matter what others say or do, they will admire you for it.

CHRISTINA WOODS
EIGHTH GRADE

I hope very much that I will live a life that is full of love and thrills. I want little bumps on my road of life.

ELIZABETH ROULSTON
SIXTH GRADE

My first hope is;
I hope This world
would be
a better
place whe
my children are
my age.

Chapter Five

Let the world

celebrate

together.

Hope Bennett
SECOND GRADE

stand for
something

more than
yourself

Children inevitably dream of making life better for others as well as for themselves. Girls and young women care deeply for the web of community in which they grow up, and they hope for the ability to right wrongs, to solve problems, to cure ills. Women such as Marian Wright Edelman, president of the Children's Defense Fund, and Nadine Strossen, president of the American Civil Liberties Union, have committed themselves to working towards a better world, and they urge their young readers to include this goal in their dreams. Leave "a legacy of conscience and caring," urges Edelman, and Sixth Grader Hanna responds, "I want everyone to have equal opportunities, no matter what they look like or where they come from or live."

We are living at an incredible moral moment in history. Few human beings are blessed to anticipate or experience the beginning of a new century and millennium. How will we say thanks for the life, earth, nation, and children God has entrusted to our care? What legacies, principles, values, and deeds will we send to the future – through our children to their children and to a spiritually confused, balkanized, and violent world desperately hungering for moral leadership?

How will progress be measured over the next thousand years if we survive them? By the kill power and number of weapons of destruction we can produce and traffic at home and abroad or by our willingness to shrink, indeed destroy, the prison of violence constructed at home and abroad in the name of peace and security? By how many material things we can manufacture, advertise, sell, and consume or by our rediscovery of more lasting, non-material measures of success – a new Dow-Jones for the purpose and quality of life in our families, neighborhoods, and national community? By how rapidly technology and corporate mergermania can render human beings and human work obsolete or by a better balance between corporate profits and corporate caring for children, families,

and communities? By how much a few at the top can get at the expense of the many at the bottom and in the middle or by our struggle for a concept of enough for all Americans?

The answers lie in the values, decisions, and actions we stand for today. What an opportunity for good and evil we Americans personally and collectively hold as parents, citizens, community leaders, and as titular world leader in the post-cold war and postindustrial era on the cusp of the third millennium.

In the United States since 1979, more than 60,000 children have been killed by guns in our homes, schools, and neighborhoods in a civil war on our young. In the richest nation in history, we appear unashamed that a child dies from poverty every 53 minutes, that children are the poorest group of Americans; and we do not express outrage as political leaders of both parties propose policies to make them poorer. We talk about family values, but turn our backs on real needs of families for jobs and decent wages and child care and health care. We tolerate a child welfare system that abuses and neglects children already abused and neglected by their families.

How much suffering, death, and neglect will it take for you and me and religious, civic, community, and political leaders to stand up and cry out "Enough" with our hearts and voices and votes to protect and ensure fair treatment for our young who are our sacred trust and collective American future?

What you and I stand for and do now for our children, or fail to do, will determine our nation's fate in the new century and millennium. I hope you will stand for something more than yourself, work for something more lasting than money, and leave your children and communities and nation a legacy of conscience and caring, not just distinguished careers. I hope you will take family life seriously and exercise citizenship vigilantly. I hope you will make a difference. Godspeed.

MARIAN WRIGHT EDELMAN
Founder and president,
Children's Defense Fund

One day I remember my dad and I were walking out of the parking lot of our favorite restaurant. Somehow we got to talking about all of the things that have changed since my grandfather was little. Then my dad said something that filled my mind with curiosity. He said that when I grow up, even more things will have changed, since technology is moving along so fast.

 Sometimes I stop and think, 'What could possibly change that we don't have now?' Maybe some people will be able to fly to Pluto or live in outer space permanently. I guess what I would want to happen in the future is that everyone would be able to feel loved and well cared for instead of never having any conversation with their family and growing up hating their parents. I also want everyone to have equal opportunities, no matter what they look like or where they come from or live. I wish that all the problems with Iraq would be solved and no one would have to worry about wars. When I grow up, I would like to be a fourth-grade teacher and someday have a family. Then, walking out of my child's and my favorite restaurant, I would tell them all that has changed since I was young, just like my dad told me.

HANNA MANNING
SIXTH GRADE

I wish that a world with violence against women will someday be something studied as an anomaly of the past. How wonderful to have a world in which girls and women don't think twice about walking through a park alone, going freely into the night to explore their worlds. A hundred years from now, perhaps all parents will feel at peace in letting their children gain independence bit by bit because they can trust the adults around them, friend or unknown, to keep a watchful eye on each and every child.

I hope for a world where everyday language is respectful of each human, male or female, whatever color or religion. In our own country, I hope it takes far less than 100 years for us to allow each person to find their full human potential in their work and in their life with friends and family.

I hope for an America in which every citizen accepts her responsibility to understand our history and to be an informed participant in our decision making. I hope for an America in which everyone pays attention to election issues, ignores hyperbole, and most of all, votes.

I hope for an America that is like my New Mexico in its appreciation for people of many cultures, celebrating our joyous differences while working to strengthen our far more common bonds.

I dream of a world in which there are no hungry or unwanted or unreared children, a world where we have clean skies and enough food. I dream of a world which reveres art and artists, the makers of justice, and the makers of cookies.

What I believe is that great girls and wonderful boys 100 years from now will live in an America in which the elegance of human potential is almost matched by the elegance of human relationships and human accomplishment. Maybe in a world which turns the mountains rosy many nights and follows with bright stars, these ideas won't need to be dreams because they will be a reality.

ROBERTA COOPER RAMO
Past president, American Bar Association

Margaret Mead defined a perfect culture as one in which there was a place for every human gift. That is what I want for girls, a place in which they can grow and develop into all they can be and in which they are loved and respected for all their gifts.

I want girls to be valued for their character, their intelligence and their talents, not just their attractiveness and sexuality. I would like to see all shapes and sizes of women valued. In fact I would like to see women loved for their inner spirits, much more than their outer appearance.

I hope that girls born in the next century can have the kind of fun I had as a girl. That is, I hope they can find prairies to lie down in, creeks to wade and fish in and trees to crawl up into and read. I hope we have preserved great stretches of the natural world so that every girl can have the experience of wilderness deep in her bones.

MARY PIPHER, PH.D.
Clinical psychologist and author

I hope that

they will

stop killing

endangered species

and stop cutting

down the rainforest.

The white tigers

are already extinct.

Birds have

nowhere to live.

ELIZABETH SMITH
FIRST GRADE

My hopes and dreams for girls are the same as my hopes and dreams for boys. I want all of them – no matter who they are, and no matter what pigeonholes society may put them into (for example, in terms of their race, national origin, religion, sexual orientation, political beliefs, economic circumstances, and so forth) – to have fair and equal opportunities to learn and to develop their full potential.

Unfortunately, evidence now shows that this hope is far from today's reality in many respects. For example, poorer neighborhoods often have substandard public schools, and many young people who live there also can't afford to attend private schools. And too many girls are relatively ignored by their teachers, and subjected to constricting gender stereotypes – for instance, that they aren't as good as boys in math and science – which then become self-fulfilling prophecies. Of course, the girls who are fortunate enough to attend Laurel School don't have these problems. I hope that many of them might use their own excellent educational opportunities to seek similar opportunities for other young people.

I also hope that young people will be respected by their parents, teachers, and government officials as individuals who are entitled to certain basic rights, especially as they mature and approach the age of majority. Again, alas, this dream departs from current reality in important ways. Twenty years ago, the U.S. Supreme Court noted that constitutional rights "do not…come into being magically only when one attains the state-defined age of majority." Yet, since then the Court has cut back on young people's rights, including the core rights of free speech and personal privacy. Moreover, many new laws are restricting young people's access to major communications media, such as the Internet. While these restrictions claim to "protect" minors, in fact they deprive young people not only of their liberty, but also of access to much vitally important information and expression.

Although much progress has been made in the recent past, our society and our legal system still reflect and perpetuate negative stereotypes about both young people and females. Accordingly, girls are often doubly stigmatized. When my dreams come true, these stereotypes will have vanished, and every girl – along with every boy – will be respected as a unique individual.

NADINE STROSSEN
President, American Civil Liberties Union

As the human community enters the new millennium, I stand firm in my conviction that the contributions of women in all facets of life will play an increasingly central and vital role.

The greatest gift in life is that of free choice, and commensurate with that, free choice tempered with a sense of responsibility to our families, our community and our society.

Girls of today are privileged to live in a time of unprecedented opportunity and challenge. Our families are being redefined. The roles of men and women in families are being redefined. The definition of community is changing, and society itself is becoming truly global for the first time in human history.

In this time of epochal change, it is my hope that each of us will live with the intent to improve the human condition in whatever special and unique way we can. It is my hope that the girls of today take more active leadership roles in redefining the family, in redefining the community and in broadening our sense of society. The task ahead must include ensuring that our ever more crowded world includes increasing respect for tolerance, compassion and patience.

It is my dream that you will find, as I have, that the greatest blessings and deepest rewards in life come from helping others, from giving to those in need, and from striving to care for the world in which we are merely guests.

As those of us now carrying the mantle of leadership prepare to pass this to you, it is my wish to each of you personally that you will lead with conviction, with warmth and an open heart, and that you will strive to bring love into every act.

BENAZIR BHUTTO
Former Prime Minister of Pakistan

I don't quite know what I want to be. All I have is an outline. I know that, like Miss Rumphius, "When I grow up, I want to go to faraway places and when I grow old, I want to live beside the sea." But my main goal is to "make the world more beautiful."

GRACE D'ADDIO
SIXTH GRADE

I truly hope that by the time I graduate from college (2008), the world will be a better place. There would be no homeless, and there would be no difference between rich and poor. I hope that by then, money will have no meaning and we will all get things free.

There would be:

No kings, no queens.

No princesses, no princes.

No crimes, no guns.

No cheaters, liars.

Or bad lawyers.

Actually, no lawyers.

No wars, only peace.

Friendship, happiness.

No worries.

Everyone loves each other.

No suicide.

It seems odd, doesn't it? Others may want to be rich, and swim in a pool full of diamonds and riches. But I don't want to. Sure, I sometimes want foolish things, like marrying movie stars and expanding my wardrobe ten thousand times, but that's not important. I would also like something that I know won't be possible. I want children to get an excellent education. A good education that you don't have to pay for. Most public schools don't even compare to Laurel's education. I think that is unfair. Just because the parents don't have money doesn't mean that the child is dumb. It is very unfair and very wrong.

INGRID ROSIUTO
SIXTH GRADE

Chapter Six

Become

the first

woman

President.

Victoria Pullella
SECOND GRADE

make the world
a better place

Will the world be a better place when the girls of today are grown? So many of the contributors in this book have made it their goal to improve the world for future generations. The opportunities open to girls now, and the richness of girls' dreams about the future, are proof that the hard work of women leaders has made an impact. But more is still to be done, and the women featured in this chapter encourage girls to dedicate their talents to the challenge of creating a better world. The late U.S. Ambassador Pamela Harriman urges, "Define who you are, and then help others to live in peace and dignity." Journalist Christiane Amanpour asks girls "to be prepared to sacrifice, to strive for what's right instead of what's easy." And young Rebecca replies, "I'll take a risk./ I'll be a peacemaker./I'll help out."

We must do everything in our power to encourage girls to believe in themselves, believe in each other, and seek as individuals and members of a larger community the fulfillment of their dreams.

When I was a girl, women rarely participated in public affairs. Today, that has all changed. Women are increasingly present at all levels of local, state, national and even international affairs.

When I was your age, I did not set myself the goal of being an Ambassador. That was not, at that time, an acceptable ambition. My dreams were to find my own way, to learn as much as possible from other people, and to use that knowledge to serve a larger community. My hope was to work to defend the values of democracy, which were under attack during the Second World War and the Cold War, and to work for social justice and human dignity.

Now, as Ambassador to France, I have a wonderful opportunity to make a difference. I hope that I might also be able to set an example for young girls. We should have the confidence to pursue our individual ambitions, but I believe deeply that we realize our full potential as people and as citizens only when we contribute to something larger. It does not have to be the government; it can be any field which ignites our passionate interest. I would say to girls, "Define who you are, and then help others to live in peace and dignity." That is a dream worth dreaming.

PAMELA HARRIMAN
U.S. Ambassador to France

Maybe I can be a lawyer, to help people have fair, truthful justice. Maybe I will become a lawyer to help one person have the same advantage or to save one accused life.

Maybe I will become a teacher to help children learn and have an impact on their lives so they can learn to get along with many others and can become successful. Maybe I will become a teacher just to help one child.

Maybe I will become a dancer to bring fun and entertainment into people's lives. Maybe I can become a dance teacher and teach a student so she can get a scholarship and become the prima ballerina I never became.

Maybe I will work with the Salvation Army, or the Peace Corps and help needy children and adults eat and stay warm.

Then I will know that I have put my life to good use.

SYDNEY SAFFOLD
SIXTH GRADE

As the first Democratic woman to be elected to the United States Senate in her own right, I know that girls can grow up to do whatever they want. This one did. It is important that you know that, too. You are our inspiration for today and our promise for tomorrow.

I began my political career 25 years ago by organizing my neighborhood to stop construction of a 16-lane highway through a historic area of Baltimore. I saw an injustice and I got involved. I urge you to do the same. Get involved in your community, volunteer for a cause you care about, make a difference. It is our responsibility to make this a better world.

I hope you also learn to measure your success not by glitz or glory but by how you practice the habits of the heart – by being a good friend, a good neighbor, and a good citizen.

In my career in the Senate, I have made every effort to open the doors of opportunity for you. I have made sure that math and science classes are available and accessible to girls. Now you can be the scientist who finds the cure to cancer or the astronaut who explores new frontiers of space. I didn't open the doors of opportunity to let the breeze in, I opened it to let more girls in. I will continue to open doors – it's up to you to walk right through!

Just look at all the differences women have made. We make a difference in our homes, in our communities, and in our country. We have made a difference in the Senate. We don't just bring heels to the corridors of power. We bring a new perspective and new solutions. And, we bring heels for you to fill.

It's my hope that someday, one of you will become the President of the United States. One of you might find the cure for AIDS or breast cancer. Many of you will be mothers. You will all be a success. I have faith in the future because I believe in you – in your optimism, your energy, and your capacity to achieve. You can do whatever you want. I did.

BARBARA A. MIKULSKI
U.S. Senator from Maryland

Aspire, and work hard to achieve your aspirations. Appreciate that, in our open society, no doors are closed to people willing to spend the hours of effort needed to make dreams come true. And leave tracks. Just as others have been way pavers for your good fortune, so you should aid those who will follow in your way. Think of your children and grandchildren to come, and do your part to make society as you would want it to be for them.

RUTH BADER
GINSBURG
*U.S. Supreme Court
Justice*

I hope I will
be a teacher
to help
people learn.
It's good to
help people
learn. You
teach math,
you teach how
to write and
to do cursive.

LEAH SILVER
SECOND GRADE

I have two dreams for girls in the next century. One is that you live in a world that is increasingly peaceful, prosperous, and free. The other is that when you grow up, you will have an equal opportunity to participate in the building of this better world. When I was a school girl, it seemed far-fetched to think of achieving either of these goals. Today, however, we have made great progress towards realizing both of them.

I was born in Czechoslovakia in 1937. The global economy was still in the throes of the Great Depression, creating unemployment and poverty for millions of families around the world. In Asia, aggression had led to the outbreak of war. And in Europe, Hitler was developing his evil plans. In the ensuing years, my family fled our homeland twice — first from the Nazis and later from the Communists. We ended up in the United States in 1948, settling in Colorado. In America, I not only had the privilege of growing up in a free society, but I learned first-hand the importance of the United States to the world. Through America's leadership in the long Cold War, democracy has triumphed over dictatorship, ushering in a new era of peace and prosperity.

When I was growing up, the world offered few opportunities for women to play active roles outside of the home. Although the suffragettes had won for women the right to vote in many Western countries, we still faced much discrimination when trying to obtain a higher education or to enter the professional and business worlds. But through the tremendous efforts of women everywhere, we have surmounted countless obstacles during the last half-century. My career is a testament to these new vistas. I have raised three daughters, attended college and graduate school, taught in a university, and served as America's Ambassador to the United Nations and now as Secretary of State. No doubt, many glass ceilings still need to be broken, but the world today offers girls and women unprecedented freedom to develop their full potential.

I wish all of you happiness and success in your lives. I dearly hope that your generation will finish the work that mine has begun. Then you must think up new dreams that your own children can reach for. Good luck!

MADELEINE ALBRIGHT
U.S. Secretary of State

My dream
is that
I finish my
dyslexia
story
so that
other
students
and
teachers
can
understand
what it is
like to
be different.

DANA BRUCK-SEGAL
FOURTH GRADE

My wish for you is that you will continue your education in order to become responsible and caring citizens. You have special talents and abilities, and you can make a difference for the better – at home, at school, in your place of worship, and in your community. Becoming involved in these areas is an important first step toward building a better America.

BARBARA BUSH
Former First Lady

Surely the women of the 20th century have greater opportunities to participate fully in our community decision-making than our sisters of the 19th century. But we have a ways to go. For you, our sisters of the 21st century, we wish full participation at every level of community life. The 21st century should bring more women governors and a woman President of the United States.

My hopes for you are:

- that you have found a way to campaign on the issues without negative personal attacks dominating the media and driving voters into apathy and despair;

- that you have created new ways to work outside the home while still cherishing the special bonds of family – nurturing children and caring for the elderly – and that all of these jobs are shared by men and women alike; and

- that you have developed strong ties across the historic divisions of race, economic status, and national origin so that every talent of all our citizens can be used.

Meet the challenges with joy, love and honesty. The world will be a better place because you made your own special contribution.

JANE L. CAMPBELL
Cuyahoga County Commissioner

HELP OUT!

Be the one.

Be in charge.

Take a risk.

Be a peacemaker.

Help out.

Be nice to the poor.

Because I believe in you.

You can do it.

But what about me?

Me Rebecca Allen?

Well.

I'll be the one.

I'll be in charge.

I'll take a risk.

I'll be a peacemaker.

I'll help out.

I'll be nice to the poor.

Because I can do it.

I believe in myself.

I'm a super helper.

And I will save the world with my super goodness.

Rebecca Allen
Third Grade

One of the most important things to learn in life is that you can make a difference in your community no matter who you are or where you live. I have seen so many good deeds — people helped, lives improved — because someone cared. Do what you can to show you care about other people, and you will make our world a better place.

ROSALYNN CARTER
Former First Lady

We women know now that we can be any-one, do anything. The question is who do we want to be, what do we want to do? My hope is that every girl will choose to try to make a difference, to make the world a better place through her endeavours, to have dreams, to embrace a mission, to be prepared for sacri-fice, to always strive for what's right instead of what's easy, to understand her special role and responsibility in our world.

CHRISTIANE AMANPOUR
Chief international correspondent,
Cable News Network

I plan to be an architect, in more than one way. I don't want just to build buildings, I want to help people by building up their self-esteem and their happiness. I want to make everyone happy with their lives. I want someone who has just lost their job to think that it will all work out in the end.

JACQUELYN CRANDELL
SIXTH GRADE

equal

Chapter Seven

Some day I hope I can be a doctor like my dad.

Alexandra Reese
KINDERGARTEN

opportunities
& boundless ambitions

Some voices in this chapter are voices strengthened and nourished 30 years ago by the birth of the movement to expand women's rights. Many successful women today acknowledge that much progress has been made in addressing gender-related inequities and prejudices that were considered acceptable just a generation ago. Younger voices, such as that of Twelfth Grader Brooke, see many obstacles that still must be overcome before girls and women are considered the equals of boys and men. The letter writers here encourage their youthful counterparts to keep on working for the equality that has been so fervently sought – equality in the workplace, equality in opportunities for leadership, equality in quality of life. As author Isabel Allende writes, "My generation made the leap, our daughters have the task of consolidating the changes and reaching out to every corner of this planet."

My hope for young women – my daughters and granddaughters and everyone else's – is that they live and flourish in a world that recognizes their needs, their talents, their ability to compete and contribute and the uniqueness of their being and their perceptions of the world.

Many pioneers have worked hard in this century to open closed doors and break through glass ceilings for young women so that they can attend schools and colleges of their choice, enter professions and get jobs for which they are qualified, vote and hold high elected and appointed offices alongside men. That goal is still a work in progress. But beyond that, I hope young women can feel freer in the next century to be and do things that are special to their gender, to bear and nurture children, express through the arts, literature and politics their visions of what society should be, without forfeiting their hard-won rights to equal treatment in those spheres where gender has no claim to recognition.

Women do have distinct aspirations, experiences and feelings and their lives should not be forced into an "either/or" choice between a fulfilling public and private persona. I hope they will not become clones content to act just like men as their numbers increase in the important parts of our national life – business, medicine, academia, the law, and the arts. I hope they will work together to create a workplace where they and their male counterparts can take time off from busy careers to stay home with young children if they so choose, and where family life will become a true priority, not a campaign slogan.

Most of all, I want young women to know from the start that the pattern of their lives is really a creation of their own – parents, spouses, children and loved ones will add immeasurably to its course – but in the final analysis what happens to them and how they handle it will depend on their own resources, reactions, attitudes and energy; they are the leading ladies in their own drama, not supporting players in some else's. That is a lesson my own generation of women learned the hard way.

When they are young I wish for them to be esteemed, to have strong role models, to be told, "Look around, women can be and do anything."

I wish for someone to show them empathy so they can grow to be empathetic women.

I wish for them a circle of loving friends, knowledge and trust in God. I wish them faith in themselves that they can always manage to work through their problems, and an appreciation of every day of their lives.

We are healers and athletes, artists, scientists and mothers. We are equal; I wish them an unblinking acceptance in that truth.

JULIEANN L. KRONE
Thoroughbred racing jockey

To the Class of 2011:

One of my many hopes for you is that you will all have equal opportunities and boundless ambitions. I would love for all of you to be able to be whatever you want to be.

It is also my hope that you will be able to bring peace to our world. It is time that people recognize the strengths and abilities that girls have.

Finally, I hope that each one of you will know how important and beautiful you are. Having grown up surrounded by a society that taught girls that beauty is only on the outside, I wish that all of you will be loved for who you are and not for what you have or how you look.

BROOKE KENNEDY
TWELFTH GRADE

My vision for young women is that they should continue to act upon gains that have been wrought by the feminist movement in terms of entering fields they never dreamed they could before and achieving spectacular results in any field they do enter, not based on special privilege or "let's make up for disparities in the past by now giving women special consideration," but just through their own energy, drive, need, intelligence and hard work. I believe that "insecurity" goes with the territory for both young men and women in terms of feeling adequate, beautiful, attractive, popular and just downright "okay" some of the time – goes with the territory of being human. I would wish that any young woman would realize she is beautiful and smart and attractive enough to be beloved and also to make a difference in the world. It doesn't have to be the whole world, just the world that she occupies while always reaching out to help others achieve their goals. Repeat: There is something every young woman can do better than others and I would wish for her to find out what that is, possibly after years of testing a lot of possibilities, and then go for it and see it happen!

HELEN GURLEY BROWN
Magazine editor and author

My hope and dream for the future of girls – and in this I include my daughter Katie – is that they will enjoy a world where all opportunities are open to them. We have come closer to having that world, but we are obviously not there yet. Every girl should know that her ambitions can be boundless. She can be president, a priest or a fighter pilot.

In addition, I hope that it will be a world where women's health issues are taken seriously and researched. I hope girls in the future will be able to talk about breast cancer as a historical problem, much the way my generation speaks of polio. I hope they will be able to focus instead on wellness and healthy living, rather than on combating disease.

Finally, I hope that our girls will be the ones who will be able to bring about peace and a just society for everyone. I have no doubt in my mind that they are capable of fixing the world and I hope that adults around them will get out of their way!

SUSAN M. LOVE, M.D.
Breast cancer specialist

To the Class of 2011:

I am headed down a long and hopefully fulfilling road of college and career opportunities, and I am sure I will encounter all types of barriers, from those regarding my educational background, to those regarding the way I look, to those regarding the fact that I am a woman. It is unrealistic to expect that in 14 years, the graduation class of 2011 will not be looking out on the same types of barriers in their future.

Rather than to wish that all these things would go away, because that will never happen, my wish is that the class of 2011 will be endowed with the strength I hope that I have, the strength to overcome these barriers, to break down these walls, and to conquer these stereotypes by virtue of their own personalities and achievements. Breaking down walls gives a person meaning, gives a person strength. So I do not wish for walls to never rise. I only wish that those in the class of 2011, and all the classes before and after them, will be able to gain victory over the barriers they encounter.

MARGARET FAIRMAN
TWELFTH GRADE

My hopes and dreams for girls were primarily developed and nurtured by Laurel School, The Junior League of Cleveland, Inc., and the Cleveland Foundation. However, because of my advantaged youth, I was in my late thirties before I realized that being a woman did not provide me with equal rights under the law – that, in fact, around the world, all women suffered from the results of prejudice and institutionalized perceived inferiority.

The battle for equal rights continues unabated, as it should for all people. However, about two years ago I realized that the acquisition of legal rights could never be the ultimate solution for equal opportunity, and that the effective and meaningful implementation of legal rights in a democracy must be accompanied by a dedicated commitment to personal responsibility. And so with great enthusiasm, I proceeded to write down what I thought some of these personal responsibilities might be. They included:

- the pursuit of knowledge and the ethical and moral use of that knowledge;

- the development of one's special talents and potential;

- the maintenance of good physical and mental health by preventing problems that can be avoided;

- the development of financial and economic well-being;

- the respectful maintenance of one's home and the environment;

- the commitment to a civil society which includes voting, voluntary civic service, the monitoring of justice, freedom of choice, and reaching out to those in need; and

- the commitment to love and care wisely for a man, woman or child, or even another creature.

Obviously the list could continue, with responsibilities that pertain to all people, but I also believe that girls and women have special responsibilities because they are the only gender that can give birth to a child. Furthermore, because of the development of highly successful contraceptives, a rather recent empowerment, most females can decide whether or not, and when, to give birth. This means that girls and women can and should be personally responsible for the use of their bodies, and for nurturing and protecting the children to whom they give birth, and for ensuring that each child receives the best possible education until reaching adulthood. I also believe that girls and women need to understand, feel comfortable with, and even cherish their femaleness and the specialness of the female body and female brain.

I have not yet fulfilled all the items on my list of responsibilities, but hopefully, I still have time to do so. My hopes and dreams for young girls are that, from an early age, they will appreciate and cherish the rights and privileges that already exist and that through the acceptance of personal responsibilities they will develop their opportunities for knowledge, power, equality and love.

GWILL LINDERME YORK NEWMAN
Civic activist and
Laurel School Distinguished Alumna

I wish for every girl the freedom and opportunity to do good work of great personal interest and societal importance — the chance to make a real contribution and to derive immense satisfaction from having done so. I wish as well for each girl, a personal or family circumstance that reinforces, enhances, balances or blends compatibly with such a life of giving of oneself both personally and professionally. I know of no greater rewards than these.

ELLEN V. FUTTER
President,
American Museum
of Natural History

I want
to take
the world
by storm,
letting it
know I
am here
to stay.

GWEN
HASHIMOTO
SIXTH GRADE

to **express ourselves** from the

Chapter Eight

Keep on

trying until

you get it.

Elizabeth Kinkopf
SECOND GRADE

inside out

While acknowledging the help and support of others, the contributors in this chapter remind us of the importance of developing one's inner being, one's character. We have been hearing a lot recently – in the media, in research reports and in parenting books – about the fact that girls are more vulnerable than boys during certain developmental stages. But the inner strength and tenacity of these prominent women, and of girls who dream of making a difference, show us that a young woman's vulnerability can be mastered. These writers have looked deep inside themselves for answers to life's questions and struggles, and now they urge girls of the next generation to discover and cherish the integrity that lies within each of them. Observes educator Marva Collins, "The greatest strength I have has been my sense of self."

Have a dream: A vision, not just of what you want to do, but of who you want to be, regardless of the final path you take. Remember that you will never achieve more than you dream for!

Work hard: Bringing a dream into actuality is still 90% hard work. In fact, life is hard work whatever you do, so choose your personal vision wisely. And strive with joy! It is wonderful for your health.

Don't be afraid to fail: We all suffer defeats. But if you do not risk failure, you will never see victory. Without courage, vision means nothing and goodness is only theoretical. But courage comes easily when you direct it toward an important, greater good.

Never forget what you believe in: Don't lose your moral center; when you stand for something, be sure it expresses who you are and who you wish to be.

Whatever you do, do it as a woman: Sometimes women, even today, feel that to achieve they must be and act like men. Don't buy into that notion! Decide the important life choices on their merits, not by any standard that doesn't fit you.

Be a mentor: Be a good guide for those who come along behind you. Whatever your age, share what you have learned: as a big sister, as an upperclassman or as a good advisor to a friend. Women must help other women. Start now!

Don't ever forget your loved ones: As a physician I have been privileged to share the most profound moments of people's lives, including their final moments. And at the end, what counts is who they loved and who loved them: their families, their friends. That circle of love is everything, and a good measure of a life — of whether you made a difference, of the risks you took and the courage you expressed.

BERNADINE HEALY, M.D.
Dean of the College of Medicine and Public Health
at The Ohio State University

Walk every extra mile, take nothing for granted, be ready for life's surprises, strengthen yourself in every way, follow your intuition but learn from experience, find your balance, know yourself, never quit if it matters, be grateful, but above all, love much. Woman is The Great Preserver, and the one who will keep this planet alive and blessed for millenniums to come. So be a humble light unto others, illuminate new paths. Live joyfully; this is your time.

GISÈLE BEN-DOR
*Orchestra conductor
and music director*

To the Class of 2011:

To achieve your hopes and dreams I give you these guidelines.

1. Love and respect your mother. You'll need her more than you can imagine.

2. Try to define who you want to be and be that person. Remember, however, that to mature is to constantly reevaluate yourself.

3. Give people your respect until they prove you shouldn't.

4. Do what makes you happy, but try not to harm other people. Follow your dreams, never anyone else's. Other people's dreams will never make you happy.

5. Fall in love with someone at least once.

ADRIENNE THOMPSON
TWELFTH GRADE

I started Seventh Grade as an optimistic girl, ready for anything, except what was coming. All of a sudden I was behind in my work. I was getting Bs and Cs in practically all my classes. I know that doesn't sound too terrible, but I was used to getting As. I hated school so much I wanted to quit. Some nights I would cry myself to sleep. Everything was wrong, nothing went right.

I knew I had to talk to someone, so I decided that the person would be my advisor. There was only one problem: most of my homework was from her. So we talked about how I could manage my time better. I still had a lot of homework, but I wasn't up until all hours of the night. By the end of the second trimester I had mostly As and A-minuses. It was a major accomplishment for me. I smiled daily and I was socializing with my friends. I was in the swing of things again, and having fun.

The third trimester was the absolute best. I learned how to play lacrosse; I was caught up in all my subjects, and I had so many friends I didn't know what to do with all of them! My final grades were ones I will remember for a long time to come. I got all As.

I felt so proud. Not only because I had survived Seventh Grade, but also because I had gotten through the rough times. That made me stronger and able to relate to other people. The point I want to make is that anything and everything you endure will be rewarding.

SARAH SPRAGUE
EIGHTH GRADE

Growing up on the West Side of Cleveland, I was fortunate enough to have been surrounded by family members, coaches and teachers who gave me strong support and guidance – caring adults who patted me on the back, prodded me to do right, helped me to try harder and, always, to do better. It must be the same for every girl in America.

That is why, my greatest hope for all girls is that they will have the support, opportunity and self-confidence they need to fulfill their own dreams and help others to fulfill theirs. I hope that every girl has the courage to always stand up for what she believes in; the integrity to set a high standard for herself and others to follow; and most of all, I hope that every girl takes to heart the responsibility – the lifelong responsibility – to leave our world a little better than she found it.

Whether you dream of becoming an athlete or an artist, a teacher or President of the United States, I hope that you will always strive to reach your every goal, no matter what it may be. And, I hope that you will always take time to teach, mentor and pass on to every generation of girls the gifts that you have been given.

DONNA E. SHALALA
U.S. Secretary of Health and Human Services

Like my mom, I plan to be a successful and well-known woman who helps others. Also, I want to be a vet and help animals. I want to graduate from a great school, get married and have children.

I have many other little plans right now, like keeping my grades, and growing friendships with others, and being responsible and organized. Other than all that, I am satisfied and happy with my life so far.

ALLISON CHAN
SIXTH GRADE

I hope that in the future, each girl and woman will believe in her own
unique value and strength, because we will be living in a world
that nurtures them. Since an inner disbelief and emptiness is
the cause of our inability to honor ourselves and others –
and the reason women turn to dependence and men to
domination, as the culturally prescribed way to fill that
emptiness – I believe this is the only permanent path
to a peaceful, respectful, and interdependent world.
So I hope more of our education will help us to express
ourselves from the inside out, at least enough to balance
that part of education that must come from outside in.
Then we will all be teachers as well as students.

GLORIA STEINEM
Women's rights activist and author

To the Class of 2011:

My dream

is that we learn to value

more than simply the surface features

which define the individual,

but that our sense of beauty reaches to

the internal features of a person's mind and soul.

This dream

is a distant point of light

which will take some time to discern

in the confusion of a world which loves to hate.

Be proud

of who you are,

love yourself

and then you will be able to see clearly

that there is a reason to love and appreciate others.

JENNIFER DOWLING
TWELFTH GRADE

You are fortunate to be growing up in a time when women have the opportunity to bring crucial insight and a unique perspective to all levels in the public and private sectors. Thanks to the pioneering efforts of women such as First Lady Eleanor Roosevelt, the Women Airforce Service Pilots of World War II, and others, women are able to reach goals that were previously unattainable. I feel very proud to be the first woman Attorney General. We can all take pride in the innumerable contributions women make to their families, their professions, our communities and our world.

My mother taught my brothers, sister and me the saying, "Good, better, best. Don't ever rest until good is better and better is best." I encourage you to believe in yourselves and your ability to do anything you want to do, if it is the right thing to do; to always say what you believe to be right, not what you think others want to hear you say; and to study hard and seek justice for all.

JANET RENO
U.S. Attorney General

Time being the inexplicable raw material of everything, I would encourage every girl and woman to make use of every moment to fire the imagination, and steel the will, in pleasure and in pain; to know that every life must be chiseled by us, and that no life is ever served us on proverbial platters, and that God is not some cosmic bellboy put into the sky to come at our beck and call. Each of us must be willing to make many a sharp incision on the blocks given us in life; we can never depend on others to do the carving for us.

The greatest strength I have has been my sense of self. I have worked to be self-motivated, self-generated, and self-propelled, and to leave no blank spaces for others to fill in. When there is a true sense of self, we are not afraid to go down roads armed with our own vision, and we are not intimidated by the criticisms of the herd whose greatest achievement is to point out where the strong stumbled.

MARVA N. COLLINS
Educator

To the Class of 2011:

Please don't fight with each other, and try to listen to all sides of an argument. Nothing ever gets done (you never grow, you never learn, you never understand and appreciate anything new) if you are always fighting.

I apologize for preaching, but I hope you understand how much more fun and beautiful the world is if you don't choke it with hatred.

ALLISON COLLINS
TWELFTH GRADE

The lessons that taught me life isn't fair have been hard.

I can remember the night when my parents told me that I was going to have a new brother or sister. I was so angry because I already had a brother and a sister and didn't want a baby in the house. If I thought I was mad then, when my parents told me I had to move up to the attic and leave my room, I blew up! Then they told me that they were redoing the entire attic for me. I immediately cheered up and said I was sorry for yelling.

I actually got excited and wanted to name the baby. When my sister was born, I was in school and my dad called to tell me the news. He told me they had named her Mia. I love my sister, and although I thought life wasn't fair, it turned out to be one of the best things that has ever happened to me. It helped me to realize that though life isn't fair, it can give you great riches.

SARAH WANG
EIGHTH GRADE

How to get
somewhere
in the world

A strategy
to survive

Be useful

Be grateful

And you
have
it made

LOUISE
BOURGEOIS
Artist

the most demanding & indispensable of all

full-time jobs

"I hope to spend more time with my mommy. (Monday is my special day with her.)

Hayley Braun
KINDERGARTEN

The authors of the letters in this chapter remind us of a role, a job, a life choice that has been central to women throughout history. Many women with successful careers today acknowledge that the most defining aspect of their lives is their role within a family as a wife and a mother. Not surprisingly, girls write endlessly about their hopes of becoming a mother, of nurturing daughters and sons. After all, the primary role model for most girls is a mother – their own mother. Supreme Court Justice Sandra Day O'Connor, speaking from experience, assures young women that they can manage the difficult task of balancing family and career. "The wind is at your back," she writes. But she also challenges the next generation to help make changes in "how our families are run, how jobs are designed, and in our cultural and institutional attitudes towards women." For Sixth Grader Bethany, being a mother and wife will fulfill her dreams, and she writes about how she plans to be successful as the mother of "three boys and two girls."

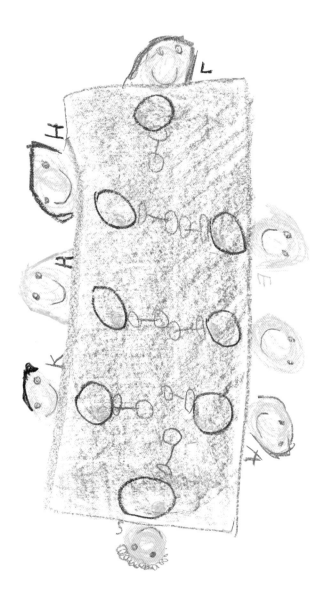

As the new millennium dawns, you can walk through any door to your dreams. Some of you will become doctors, astronauts, ministers, engineers, bankers, brokers, ambassadors, lawyers, architects, senators and CEOs.

You will find riches and renown in the future.

But some of you will be drawn to the most demanding and indispensable of all the full-time jobs open to women, what Erma Bombeck called "The Second Oldest Profession — Motherhood." It will require you to be a planner, a plumber, a playmate, a coach, a chef, a chauffeur, a nurse, a hostess, an actress, an arbitrator, an alchemist, a guard, a guide, a rule-maker, a peacemaker, a psychologist, a philosopher, a wonder worker, and a wife.

You will learn patience and flexibility and understanding. You will teach honesty, courtesy and kindness. You will receive no compensation and great condescension for this work (though it equips you to do any job in the world). But you will know the worshiping love of little children who need you so much and weather the rejection of older ones who are trying not to.

And you will shape the future.

ELAINE G. HADDEN
*Civic activist and
Laurel School
Distinguished Alumna*

Combining a career and a family is certainly not easy, but it is possible. I speak from experience as a wife and a mother of three sons. As far as I am concerned, it is worth every bit of the extra effort I put into it to have a family as well as a career. There is plenty of time to enjoy both the world of work and of the family. As for young women today, the tide is running in your favor; the wind is at your back. Women today live longer, work more, and have more opportunities to influence the direction of society than ever before in our country.

As large numbers of women enter the work force and occupy positions in politics, business, and the professions, we may have to make changes in how our families are run, how jobs are designed, and in our cultural and institutional attitudes towards women. We will have to help build the new pillars which will support our families, our jobs, and our country in the future. We will have to improvise solutions at times. They do not have to be elegant so long as they work. That is the task that the young generation will have to perform.

It is important to remember that we live in a free society and under a rule of law. Freedom means many things to different people, but most importantly it means we have the right and the responsibility to discipline ourselves. Part of that inner discipline should be a lifelong effort to leave this world a little better than you found it on your arrival. Use your talent and your education to help those who need it and in ways which will make your parents and your teachers proud of your efforts.

SANDRA DAY O'CONNOR
U.S. Supreme Court Justice

About a year ago, a friend of my Dad asked me what I want to be when I grow up. I shrugged my shoulders and gave a vague "I don't know." I still don't know what I want to do in the future, but I'm getting closer to knowing how I will do it. I want to be a mother and live in a nice house in the suburbs. But I also want a successful career. I hope if I am to be a mother, my job will not be so demanding as to make me incapable of being on the PTA or helping my children with their homework.

LAURA KLEMENT
EIGHTH GRADE

I want to have children, three boys and two girls. They will all be cool even from the day they are born. But not snobby and spoiled. They will be kind and mannerly. I won't be one of those mothers who holds their kids back, I will encourage them to push to reach their dreams.

I will be married to a confident, successful man. We won't live in a mansion but in a small cottage in a field or a nice home in Shaker Heights. It will be decorated by myself with mostly country-style furnishings. My house will represent everyone's personality and we will all agree as a family what suits us and what doesn't.

BETHANY McDANIEL
SIXTH GRADE

Nothing I've achieved in the public realm can approach the fulfillment of having a happy family life. No fame or money or victories in the public arena can compare to the joys that flow from a lifetime marriage to a good and faithful husband and the six children we raised together.

My hopes and dreams for you are that you will each find a good and faithful husband, who will love and protect you, and whose manliness will be a constant source of contentment and trust. I hope that you will then learn to face life's trials and tribulations together.

My hopes and dreams for you are that you will know the fulfillment of motherhood and how exciting it is to teach and mold a little baby as he or she grows into manhood or womanhood. Making these hopes and dreams come true takes faith and love and commitment and sacrifice and just plain hard work, but I'm here to tell you that the rewards are worth the price. And then, someday, you will know the fun of being a grandmother. It's like being born again! It's like starting life all over!

It's unfortunate that so many girls today are given a false and negative view of men, marriage and motherhood. Most of the women I've debated over the years don't have husbands or children or grandchildren. They've missed so much of life. I went to law school after I was 50 years old, but I wouldn't have wanted to have had my six children after I was 50.

In America, you have every opportunity to achieve your hopes and dreams – if you work at it. To paraphrase the theme of *It's a Wonderful Life*, no one is a failure if you have a good family life. Go to it!

PHYLLIS SCHLAFLY
President, Eagle Forum

If I grow up and have kids I would call them Fara and Tom. (If they were a girl and a boy.) If they were bad I would never spank them, but give them a time-out instead. During breakfast, lunch and dinner I would try to provide their favorite foods. I would send them to good schools. I would make sure they were the happiest kids in the world.

MARGARET MCGREW
THIRD GRADE

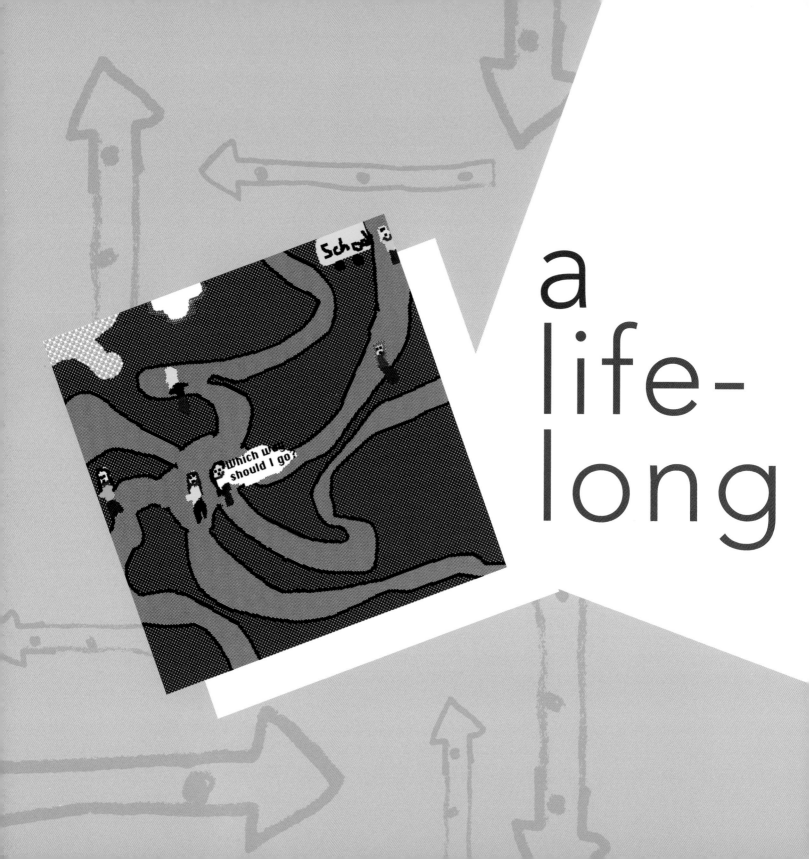

a
life-
long

Chapter Ten

Which

way

should

I go?

Michelle Lee
THIRD GRADE

love of learning

The idea for a compilation of hopes and dreams for girls and young women originated as part of the 100th anniversary celebration of a place of learning, a school that has been nurturing the love of lifelong learning in girls since it began in 1896. Those of us who teach children, who work with children daily, know that a young woman's successful pursuit of her hopes and dreams is impossible without solid preparation. The contributors in this chapter advise girls and young women to take advantage of their years in school, to "appreciate the riches offered by their education." They also remind us that the educational process is not confined exclusively to the classroom, and they show us how lessons learned from teachers, from families, from role models, from diverse experiences, helped them on their rise to prominence.

What I have been able to achieve in my life is very much a consequence of my education – as it was given to me and as I took from it, even in my earliest school days. I was fortunate to have demanding teachers who encouraged my powerful, innate desire to learn. I sought sustenance in books; I came to understand the social and political turmoil of my own times through the exploration of earlier times; I traveled, in my mind, far beyond the confines of my life. For me, education was a prize and a privilege.

My wish for girls who are growing up today is that they will appreciate the riches offered by their education while they are students rather than after; indeed, that they will value the resources, the instruction and their teachers as though their very lives depended upon it – because their lives will depend on it. Today's girls will grow up to be women in a world where they will share the same opportunities, the same responsibilities and the same challenges as men. They must have the resilience, the strength, the knowledge and the will that only education can provide. I have come to believe that throughout our lives, education is a steady presence, reassuring us of the meaning and potential of life itself. My hope for girls is that they will start very early to build that steady presence within themselves.

RUTH J. SIMMONS, PH.D.
President, Smith College

The best kind of education in my mind is to travel. To travel, to see the world, to see places far different from what you've ever seen is an education no book could sufficiently provide. I went to Costa Rica with my father and camped in the rainforest for a week with scientists who were there to do research. I can hardly describe the beauty in which orchids hung from a dense layer of foliage. Monkeys swung from branches in joyful play and parrots were as common as pigeons. When I was in the rainforest, I wanted to stay there forever.

To travel is to find out who you are.

SARA McDOWELL
EIGHTH GRADE

What promise I see in your eyes! What joy I see in your smiles! You are at the beginning of life's journey and now is the time for you to prepare for it. What will you bring with you?

I hope as you study, you will gather not only knowledge and training, but a lifelong love for learning. My years in school were wonderful and rewarding, but education need not end at graduation. There is so much we can learn throughout our lives. I hope you remember the values and ideals that are the foundation of our great country. I am so proud of our heritage and grateful to my family for instilling in me an appreciation for that legacy of faith and moral courage. My grandmother, Mom Cathey, taught me to always look for ways in my private life and professional life to make a positive difference in the lives of others. I truly believe that when we are in the service of others we not only lead a successful life but experience true joy in the journey!

ELIZABETH HANFORD DOLE
Past president, American Red Cross

When I was 10 years old, it never occurred to me that I might help to found a new national newspaper that would grow to be the largest in the country. Nor did I imagine that I could become the editor of the editorial page of that newspaper. My opportunities have come from a combination of luck, preparation and the willingness to take a gamble.

My wish for you, tomorrow's young women, is that you prepare yourselves for the luck and the gambles with careful, broad-ranging studies. Assume your challenges and opportunities will be many and exciting. Had I known the possibilities that would come my way, I would have studied more history, more politics, more geography, more literature.

In the next 100 years, I'm confident that all the differences between the kinds of jobs men and women do – and what they're paid – will vanish. You and your daughters will be able to do whatever you want. The world will need your brains to make this a better place in which to live. Find something you love to do, something that will be of service. Aim high. We'll need women presidents, women who can run companies, women who are terrific mothers, women who can fly a space craft, women who can invent computers.

And never underestimate the importance of school activities. My journalism career began in the eighth grade on my junior high school newspaper. Except for a few interruptions, I've worked for newspapers ever since.

KAREN JURGENSEN
Editorial page editor, USA Today

DAY DREAMING ON THE FIELD

My biggest dream is to be the best soccer player.

I've been following this dream since

I was three years old.

My sister says, "Forget it, you can't

even kick ten yards."

But I say "I can kick it fifty yards,"

and then I go outside and practice.

My mom says "Keep trying, Kirby,

you'll get it some day."

My dad says "If you try very

hard, you'll get it, Kirby."

I take my mom's and

dad's advice.

KIRBY FOOTE
THIRD GRADE

I dream
I am going
to be a
writer and
an artist
when I
grow up.
I will
practice
every day,
I hope.

LILLIAN YAN
FIRST GRADE

A wise man once told me: "Luck is when opportunity meets preparedness." As more and more opportunities open for women, it is important that they be as prepared as they can possibly be, and that means learning both inside and outside the classroom. I consider myself a very lucky person, but it hasn't come without a lot of hard work.

CHRISTINE
TODD WHITMAN
Governor of New Jersey

To the Class of 2011:

Know that with a fine education and determination you can do whatever you want to do.

HALLIE TRATTNER
TWELFTH GRADE

an incurable, fearless habit of

Chapter Eleven

I am curious
about what my
dad talks to
himself about
in the shower.

Emily Ritter
KINDERGARTEN

asking
questions

Why do children ask so many questions?

Adults at one time or another may lament the seemingly boundless
curiosity of children, but a child's natural fascination with the world
around her animates learning and growth and contributes to her
deeper understanding of life. Even though they encountered criticism
for doing so, the scientists whose letters are featured in this chapter held on to their childhood habit
of curiosity, and it opened up not just careers but whole worlds to them. They express our hope that
girls will never stop asking questions, even as adults, and that a "sense of wonder," as astrophysicist
Margaret Geller puts it, will always add zest and meaning to their lives.

Do you remember thinking deep thoughts when you were still so young that the furniture didn't fit you, and your legs dangled in the air? I do. One of those times, I was about five, I was sent to my room without supper and was told, "Your father will have to speak to you!" Later that evening my father came up the stairs to my room, pulled me gently onto his knee and said, "Your mother and I always tell our friends what a good little girl you are and how you would never do anything to disappoint us. Yet today you've done this terrible thing..." The terrible thing I had done was to find some beautiful red and yellow caterpillars in the garden, and, very carefully, to bring a lot of them into my room, where they so interestingly crawled all over! I realized my parents were alarmed by their strange child.

Another, much worse, problem I had was that I couldn't stop asking questions. I was often told, "It's not nice for little girls to ask questions!" I would pray at night for God to help me stop asking questions. Yet I couldn't stop.

So here it is, 65 years or more later. Ironically, I realize that what my loving parents perceived as my two worrisome flaws have constituted a main driving force in my life. As a longtime professional zoologist, as the mother of four wondrous children (wondrous even as your parents' children are wondrous!), and grandmother of fascinating grandchildren – I know that I wish for all children, all students, a lifelong devotion to the natural world we live in, with an abiding interest in and concern for all of its organisms, and an incurable, fearless (and always polite!) habit of asking questions!

I used to think that the way in which men and women look at the world about them is pretty much the same. I no longer do. In the sciences, women are apt to ask different, and very significant, kinds of questions. I think it is especially important for young women to take themselves very seriously indeed, and to ask, early on, "What kinds of questions should scientists be asking in the next century?" (It will be the Age of Biology, most scientists today aver.) "What kind of science is the most important for us to do, for our precious planet, for our fellow creatures, for human society?" It is not rash for me to predict that the fine young minds at Laurel School already include those of you who, no matter how difficult the circumstances may be, will persist in asking not only, "What can we do?" but also the tougher question, "What ought we to do?"

LOUISE
RUSSERT-KRAEMER

Zoologist

To the Class of 2011:

There are countless hopes and dreams I wish for all of you, but the dream that I believe is the most important is that you all become explorers. School is extremely important because it gives you the education and the knowledge you need in order to broaden your perspective on life. However, unless you go out and apply that knowledge, it is worthless. But it is not just important to apply the knowledge you have; it is equally or perhaps even more important that you try to find out what you don't know.

I believe that traveling is the best way to learn about yourself as well as about a foreign culture and different people. Trying new and different things and exposing yourself to a diverse group of people is also an excellent way to learn. I believe that your future experiences can be limitless as long as you never stop doing what can make all of you strong, educated and unique women, and that is exploration.

ALEXIS KING
TWELFTH GRADE

I cherish the dream that every child, girl or boy, will grow up in an environment which nurtures and preserves the sense of wonder. I hope for adequate housing, nutrition, health care, and first-rate educational opportunities for all young people regardless of family income. I hope that one day this country will have one outstanding public school system – not one system for the rich and another for the poor as we now have.

Curiosity and lifelong learning and questioning lead to the thrills of discovery and understanding. People with a sensitivity to social issues and the drive to solve challenging problems must make a richer, more humane world.

MARGARET J. GELLER, PH.D.
Astrophysicist and educator

I hope that I am a scientist and dissect things. I never did it. It will be fun.

ELISA PAMELIA
FIRST GRADE

When I grow up I want to be an astronaut or an astronomer. I think space is very interesting, and I want to find out if there is life on other planets. I also want to know if other creatures are wondering if there is life on Earth.

SHEELA PRASAD
FOURTH GRADE

I have been dreaming of being a great astronaut for as long as I can remember. I am fascinated by the mysterious worlds that lie out in this wide, vast universe. I want to know so much about it. Why is it here? Are there life forms that lie within other galaxies? I have so many questions, and the answers are unimaginable.

MAGGIE RAMSEY
EIGHTH GRADE

My dreams have changed about what I want to be when I grow up. But nothing's changed about who I want to be.

I want to be a good person. I want to always know right from wrong. I want to be kind and caring. Most of all I want to live life to the fullest.

I want to travel the world and see every famous spot there is: Connemara, Williamsburg, and the Colosseum. I want to save the whales, the rainforests, and help people less fortunate. Then I will be a sightseer and a hero.

I want to write millions of books. I will write about the world, people, places, biographies, autobiographies, poetry, science, novels, history. Then I would be an author.

I want to speed around racetracks at two thousand miles per hour. I will use every moving thing you could think of, bikes, horses, cars, skateboards, trains, and my own two feet. I want to bungee jump from the highest height, dive to the deepest depth, and land on the farthest planet. Then I will be a speedster and a daredevil.

I want to find a cure for diseases. I will cure AIDS, cancer, and Alzheimer's. I will use exotic plants that nobody's discovered, and dangerous chemicals that no one has ever dreamed of using. I will mix them together with instruments made in far off places that nobody's ever heard of. Then I will be a doctor and a lifesaver.

I want to discover and prove. I want to dig up the biggest and strongest dinosaur. I want to discover what happened to the colonists who "disappeared" from the very first settlement in Roanoke, why the dinosaurs died, and if Elvis still does live. I will find clues, and facts that everyone else will have missed. I will stand up for my ideas and no one will ever be able to prove me wrong. Then I will be a scientist and a detective.

I want to create the impossible. I will use electronics and build robots that can do everything from handy work around the house to traveling to Mars and back in fifteen seconds. I will make living birds out of old sneakers, and anything else you can possibly imagine, out of anything you want. Then I will be an inventor.

For now, though, being a hero, a sightseer, an author, a speedster, a daredevil, a doctor, a lifesaver, a scientist, a detective, and an inventor will have to wait. I'm still just a young girl writing an essay, pushing and striving for her hopes and dreams, like a hatchling still learning how to fly.

ALICIA BUSA
SIXTH GRADE

To the Class of 2011:

The most important thing is to stay educated. Read. Read newspapers, read books, talk to people. Question everything, and only accept that which you know for yourself is true.

SHEILA KELLER
TWELFTH GRADE

biographies

Biographical

information

about the

contributors

MADELEINE
ALBRIGHT

U.S. Secretary of State

The highest ranking woman in President Clinton's administration, Madeleine Albright is the first woman to be appointed Secretary of State. Prior to her appointment in January 1997, she served as the U.S. Permanent Representative to the United Nations and as a member of President Clinton's Cabinet and the National Security Council. Secretary Albright formerly was the president of the Center for National Policy and research professor of international affairs and director of the Women in Foreign Service Program at Georgetown University's School of Foreign Service.

ISABEL
ALLENDE

Novelist

One of Latin America's foremost writers, Isabel Allende brings a surrealistic style to her political fiction. Born in Peru and raised in Chile, she went into exile after her uncle, Chilean president Salvador Allende, was overthrown in 1973. Allende, now a resident of northern California, has received international praise for her novels, which include *The House of the Spirits*, *Of Love and Shadows*, *Eva Luna* and *The Infinite Plan*.

CHRISTIANE
AMANPOUR

Chief international correspondent, Cable News Network

Christiane Amanpour has been widely acclaimed for her extensive coverage of the civil unrest in Haiti, Algeria, Rwanda and Bosnia (the former Yugoslavia). Amanpour began her career at CNN in 1983 and gained a reputation as a world-class correspondent with her in-depth reporting on the dramatic changes in central Europe during 1989 and 1990. She has been awarded numerous prizes, including the Breakthrough Award from Women, Men and Media for her Gulf War reporting and George Polk Awards for Excellence in Journalism for her coverage of Bosnia in 1994 and for her work on the CNN special, "Battle for Afghanistan," in 1997.

GISÈLE
BEN-DOR

Orchestra conductor and music director

One of today's most dynamic and talented young conductors, Gisèle Ben-Dor is the music director of the Santa Barbara Symphony and the Pro Arte Chamber Orchestra of Boston. She was previously conductor of the Annapolis Symphony Orchestra, assistant conductor of the Louisville Orchestra and resident conductor of the Houston Symphony. Ben-Dor frequently performs as guest conductor for such renowned orchestras as the New York Philharmonic, the London Symphony Orchestra, the Boston Pops Orchestra, the Ulster Orchestra and the Israel Philharmonic Orchestra.

BENAZIR BHUTTO

Former Prime Minister of Pakistan

When Mohtarma Benazir Bhutto was sworn in as Prime Minister of Pakistan in October 1993, she became only the second person in her country's history to have been elected to that office twice through a popular mandate. Daughter of the late Zulifaker Ali Bhutto, a former Prime Minister of Pakistan, who was executed in 1979, she led the Pakistan Peoples Party from 1977 to 1988, waging a relentless struggle for the restoration of democracy and human rights in her homeland. In 1988, when she was first elected Prime Minister, she became the first woman to head an Islamic state. Her second term as Prime Minister ended with her party's defeat in 1997, and she is now leader of the opposition.

PATRICIA ANN BLACKMON

Administrative Judge, Court of Appeals of Ohio

In 1990, Patricia Ann Blackmon became the first African-American woman to be elected to the Court of Appeals of Ohio, Eighth Appellate District, upsetting three veteran opponents to win her first run for public office. Judge Blackmon began her legal career as a research assistant for the Victims/Witness Program in 1974 and then became assistant prosecutor for the City of Cleveland. In 1986, she was appointed the city's chief prosecutor. She briefly served the Ohio Turnpike Commission as staff attorney before running for the judiciary.

LOUISE BOURGEOIS

Artist

For the past 40 years, French sculptor, printmaker and performance artist Louise Bourgeois has maintained a unique and independent vision, exploring the image of the body to express ideas about universal questions. A resident of New York since 1938, she has exhibited around the world at museums from London to Tokyo to Seattle. The first woman to be given a retrospective by New York's Museum of Modern Art, Bourgeois has earned many awards, including the 1987 Distinguished Artist Award for Lifetime Achievement from the College Art Association and the 1997 National Medal of Arts.

HELEN GURLEY BROWN

Former magazine editor and author

In her more than 30 years as editor-in-chief of *Cosmopolitan*, Helen Gurley Brown oversaw the growth of this ground-breaking women's magazine from a circulation of less than eight hundred thousand to nearly three million as it became a national and then a worldwide sensation. For her exemplary contributions to magazine journalism, Brown was honored with the 1996 American Society of Magazine Editors' Hall of Fame Award, and she was the first woman recipient of the Magazine Publishers of America's prestigious Henry Johnson Fisher Award. Brown is the author of the best-selling books, *Sex and the Single Girl*, *Sex and the Office* and *Having it All*.

BARBARA
BUSH

Former First Lady

JANE L.
CAMPBELL

*Commissioner, Cuyahoga
County, Ohio*

ROSALYNN
CARTER

Former First Lady

JULIA
CHILD

Gourmet chef and author

Her husband's service as Vice President and President of the United States offered Barbara Bush a unique opportunity to make a difference in the life of the country, and since leaving the White House in 1993, she has continued tirelessly to serve others. Bush has worked as a volunteer for and supported hundreds of philanthropic organizations, including AmeriCares, the Mayo Clinic Foundation, the Leukemia Society of America and Ronald McDonald Houses. Her primary cause, however, remains family literacy. Author of the best-selling *Millie's Book*, whose profits benefited literacy programs, she helped to develop the Barbara Bush Foundation for Family Literacy in 1990.

Jane Campbell is one of three Cuyahoga County Commissioners representing 1.5 million people in Greater Cleveland and is president of that governing body. As commissioner for the most populous county in Ohio, she manages human services, economics and infrastructure development and redevelopment. Prior to her election, Campbell served for twelve years in the Ohio House of Representatives, where she was elected majority whip and assistant minority leader.

Former First Lady Rosalynn Carter has worked for more than two decades to improve the quality of life for people around the world. Today, she is an advocate for mental health, human rights, conflict resolution and the empowerment of urban communities through the Carter Center, a nonprofit institution founded in 1982 by Carter and her husband, former President Jimmy Carter. Maintaining a lifelong dedication to issues affecting women and children, she helped to launch a nationwide campaign in 1991 to publicize the need for early childhood immunizations.

The world's most famous chef, Julia Child is credited with revolutionizing the way Americans eat. Her countless books, starting with the landmark *Mastering the Art of French Cooking*, have sold millions of copies. For two decades her television show, "The French Chef," was a PBS mainstay. In 1980, Child was elected the first woman member of the American Chapter of the chefs' society, La Commanderie des Cordon Bleus de France, and two of her most recent television series, "In Julia's Kitchen" and "Baking with Julia," won Emmy awards.

ELEANOR
CLIFT

Contributing editor,
Newsweek

A key member of the *Newsweek* political reporting team, Eleanor Clift regularly reports for the national news magazine on the White House, Congress and the diverse personalities in Washington's power structure. She is also a television commentator on "The McLaughlin Group" and for Fox News Network. Co-author of the book, *War Without Bloodshed: The Art of Politics*, she is currently at work on a second book, *Madam President*, about the rise of women in politics. Clift has played herself in several Hollywood movies, including *Independence Day* and *Dave*, as well as in the CBS series, "Murphy Brown."

HILLARY
RODHAM CLINTON

First Lady

The First Lady headed President Bill Clinton's Task Force on National Health Care Reform. As First Lady of Arkansas for 12 years, she chaired an education committee that established public school standards in Arkansas, while working as a full-time partner of a law firm. Previously, Clinton taught on the law faculty of the University of Arkansas, served on the Impeachment Inquiry staff of the U.S. House of Representatives during its investigation of President Richard Nixon and was a staff attorney for the Children's Defense Fund.

MARVA N.
COLLINS

Educator

Hailed as a "superteacher," Marva Collins has received worldwide recognition for her success in educating "unteachable" inner-city children in her own Westside Prep school in Chicago. Following her unique educational vision, she left the Chicago public schools in 1975 to open Westside Prep, whose program accomplishments and increased enrollment led her to establish a second school on Chicago's south side. Collins and her schools have been featured on hundreds of radio and television programs, and a made-for-television movie about her life, *The Marva Collins Story*, continues to be aired worldwide.

JILL KER
CONWAY, PH.D.

Educator and historian

Jill Ker Conway was the first woman president of Smith College, a position to which she was appointed after serving as vice president of internal affairs at the University of Toronto. Since leaving Smith in 1985, she has been a visiting scholar and professor with the Program in Science, Technology and Society at the Massachusetts Institute of Technology. A noted historian, specializing in the experiences of women in America, Dr. Conway is also the author of *The Road from Coorain*, an autobiography of growing up on a sheep ranch in Australia, and *True North*, a memoir.

ELIZABETH
HANFORD DOLE

*Past president,
American Red Cross*

Elizabeth Dole has served five American Presidents and been named by the Gallup Poll as one of the world's 10 most admired women. She was president of the American Red Cross from 1991 to 1999. Previously, she was deputy assistant to the President for consumer affairs during the Nixon administration, a member of the Federal Trade Commission for five years and assistant to President Ronald Reagan for public liaison. In 1983, Dole joined President Reagan's cabinet as U.S. Secretary of Transportation. She was the first woman to hold that position. In 1989, she was sworn in by President George Bush as the nation's 20th Secretary of Labor.

MARIAN WRIGHT
EDELMAN

*Founder and president,
Children's Defense Fund*

Marian Wright Edelman founded the Children's Defense Fund in 1973, and under her leadership the Washington-based organization has become a strong national voice for children and families. The first African-American woman admitted to the Mississippi bar, Edelman directed the NAACP Legal Defense and Educational Fund Office in Jackson. She founded the Washington Research Project, a public interest law firm and the parent body of the Children's Defense Fund, and has served as the director of the Center for Law and Education at Harvard University.

GERTRUDE B. ELION
(DECEASED)

*Medical scientist and
Nobel Laureate*

Recipient of the 1988 Nobel Prize for Medicine, Gertrude B. Elion was named scientist emerita with Glaxo Wellcome Inc. after retiring as head of the department of experimental therapy in 1983. During her nearly 40-year career with Wellcome, she spearheaded the development of two of the first successful drugs for the treatment of leukemia. She also is credited with the development of azathioprine, an agent to prevent the rejection of kidney transplants. Elion, past president of the American Association for Cancer Research, was active in research and professional organizations while holding appointments as medical research professor of pharmacology and medicine at Duke University and adjunct professor of pharmacology at the University of North Carolina.

SUZANNE
FARRELL

Ballet dancer

Suzanne Farrell is a *répétiteur* for the George Balanchine Trust, the independent organization founded by heirs to the Balanchine repertory to oversee the worldwide licensing and production of his ballets. Farrell has staged Balanchine ballets all over the world, and her international tours and appearances on television and in the movies have made her one of the most recognized and highly esteemed artists of her generation. After joining Balanchine's New York City Ballet in 1961, she quickly became not only his most prominent ballerina but a symbol of that artistic era.

DONNA
FERRATO

*Photojournalist and
Laurel School
Distinguished Alumna*

A self-taught photographer, Donna Ferrato has been published extensively in *Life*, *Fortune*, *Time*, *The New York Times Magazine* and *USA Today*. For her documentation of domestic violence, she has received numerous awards, including the W. Eugene Smith Grant, the Robert F. Kennedy Award for Humanistic Photography and the Kodak Crystal Eagle for Courage in Journalism. Ferrato's book, *Living With the Enemy*, was published in 1991. Building on interest in the book, she founded the Domestic Abuse Awareness Project to raise funds and educate the public about domestic violence. She received the Laurel School Distinguished Alumna Award in 1992.

BETTY
FRIEDAN

*Women's rights activist
and author*

A prominent spokesperson for women's rights, Betty Friedan wrote *The Feminine Mystique* (1963), which has been called the catalytic work of the women's movement. Also the author of *The Second Stage* and *It Changed My Life*, Friedan founded the National Organization of Women (NOW) in 1966 and served as its first president. She has travelled and lectured internationally and has been a visiting scholar at Yale, Columbia and Cornell Universities.

ELLEN V.
FUTTER

*President, American Museum
of Natural History*

Now president of the American Museum of Natural History, Ellen Futter served as president of Barnard College from 1980 to 1993. An attorney by training, she currently serves on the boards of several prominent corporations and organizations, including Bristol-Myers Squibb Company, J. P. Morgan & Company, Phi Beta Kappa Associates and the American Ditchley Foundation. A fellow of the American Academy of Arts and Sciences and a member of the Council on Foreign Relations, Futter has been honored with the Barnard Medal of Distinction, the Gold Medal Award from the National Institute of Social Sciences and the Eleanor Roosevelt Leadership Award from NOW.

MARGARET J.
GELLER, PH.D.

Astrophysicist and educator

Margaret J. Geller is professor of astronomy at Harvard University and senior scientist at the Harvard-Smithsonian Center for Astrophysics. For more than 15 years, she has worked on ambitious surveys of the distribution of galaxies in the universe. A recipient of a MacArthur Foundation Fellowship, Dr. Geller has been widely recognized for her significant contributions to science and to science education.

RUTH BADER GINSBURG

U.S. Supreme Court Justice

Ruth Bader Ginsburg was sworn in as justice of the U.S. Supreme Court in August 1993, after serving 13 years on the bench of the U.S. Court of Appeals for the District of Columbia Circuit. She has taught on the law faculties of Columbia University, Rutgers University, University of Amsterdam, Harvard University, New York University and University of Strasbourg. Justice Ginsburg was instrumental in launching the Women's Rights Project of the American Civil Liberties Union and, in the 1970s, litigated a series of cases that solidified a constitutional principle against gender-based discrimination.

JANE GOODALL, PH.D.

Wildlife researcher and conservationist

Jane Goodall is the world's foremost authority on chimpanzees, having closely observed their behavior for more than 35 years in the jungles of the Gombe Game Reserve in Africa. Dr. Goodall's revolutionary observations and discoveries have been heralded internationally, and her extensive research and writing have advanced scientific thinking regarding human evolution. In 1977, she founded the Jane Goodall Institute for Wildlife Research, Education and Conservation to provide ongoing support of field research on wild chimpanzees.

ELAINE G. HADDEN

Civic activist and Laurel School Distinguished Alumna

Elaine Hadden has worked tirelessly for countless organizations in Cleveland, Ohio, and has served on the boards of Case Western Reserve University, United Way Services of Cleveland and the former Union Commerce Bank. In the early 1970s, as president of The Junior League of Cleveland, Inc., she spearheaded the revitalization of Cleveland's Playhouse Square Center and helped to convince city and corporate leaders to support the venerable theater complex. Hadden and her late husband, John, served as presidents of Hanna Perkins Center for Research in Child Development. She received the Laurel School Distinguished Alumna Award in 1986.

PAMELA HARRIMAN (DECEASED)

U.S. Ambassador to France

Pamela Harriman passed away in February 1997 after a distinguished career in politics and foreign service. The daughter of an English baron, she was first married to Winston Churchill's son, Randolph. After her third husband, Averill Harriman, an elder of the Democratic party, died in 1986, Mrs. Harriman took over his leadership role. She forged for herself a new identity as a political powerhouse in Washington, D.C. and helped to rebuild the Democratic party in the 1980s through aggressive fundraising. President Clinton appointed her U.S. Ambassador to France in 1993.

BERNADINE
HEALY, M.D.

*Dean of the College of
Medicine and Public Health
at The Ohio State University*

As Dean of the College of
Medicine and Public Health
at Ohio State University since
1995, Bernadine Healy has
been a leader in numerous
medical and scientific associa-
tions and has received many
awards for her accomplishments. Editor-in-chief of *The
Journal of Women's Health*, she
became medical advisor and
commentator for CBS News in
1997. Dr. Healy was chairman
of the Research Institute of
The Cleveland Clinic Foundation from 1984 to 1991, when
she became director of the
National Institutes of Health,
the major funding source for
biomedical research at universities and hospitals nationwide.

KAREN
JURGENSEN

Editorial page editor,
USA Today

Karen Jurgensen became editor
of the *USA Today* editorial
page in 1991 after two years as
senior editor/days. Joining the
national newspaper in 1982,
she served as Life Section editor, managing editor/cover
stories and then senior editor/
special projects. A career journalist, Jurgensen has served
on various committees of the
American Society of News-
paper Editors and chaired its
1994 Press, Bar and Public
Affairs Committee.

JULIEANN L.
KRONE

*Thoroughbred
racing jockey*

Julieann Krone became the
most-celebrated female jockey
in the history of horse racing.
Her record-breaking accomplishments include being the
first woman to win the
Belmont Stakes, to win five
races in one day at a New
York track and to compete in
a Breeders' Cup race. Winner
of more than $56 million in
purses, Krone has made more
than 2,800 trips to the win-
ners' circle.

SHERRY
LANSING

*Chairman,
Paramount Studios*

Chairman of the Motion
Picture Group of Paramount
Pictures since 1992, Sherry
Lansing oversees all aspects
of the company's operations.
Previously, Lansing headed
her own production company,
Lansing Productions, and
served as president of produc-
tion at 20th Century Fox.
Lansing has received myriad
honors, including the Over-
coming Obstacles Achieve-
ment Award for Business, the
YWCA Silver Achievement
Award and the Outstanding
Woman in Business Award
from the Women's Equity
Action League.

ROCHELLE (SHELLY) B. LAZARUS

Chairman and chief executive officer, Ogilvy & Mather Worldwide

Shelly Lazarus heads an advertising company with 312 offices located in 90 countries and billings of $8.3 billion in 1996. During her 25-year tenure with Ogilvy & Mather, Lazarus has held a series of significant management positions and has worked in every area of advertising. She has been recognized by Advertising Women of New York, which named her Advertising Woman of the Year in 1994.

SUSAN M. LOVE, M.D.

Breast cancer specialist

Susan M. Love is an author, teacher, surgeon, researcher and activist. In 1988, she founded the nationally recognized Faulkner Breast Centre in Boston and later was recruited by the University of California-Los Angeles to establish the Revlon/UCLA Breast Center, a comprehensive program addressing all aspects of breast care. In addition to her clinical work, Love has been a leader in developing innovative approaches to breast cancer treatment, authoring many journal articles and co-authoring the *Atlas of Surgical Techniques in Breast Surgery*.

BARBARA A. MIKULSKI

U.S. Senator from Maryland

Elected to a third term in the U.S. Senate in 1998, Barbara Mikulski is a national leader on the issue of women's health care, a champion for the rights of working people and an aggressive advocate for jobs for Maryland. In 1994, she was unanimously elected as secretary of the Democratic Conference of the 104th Congress, making her the first woman to hold a leadership position in the Senate. In her role as ranking member of the Labor and Human Resources Subcommittee on Aging, Senator Mikulski hopes to redefine and move forward an aggressive agenda on the process of aging and women's health.

MARTINA NAVRATILOVA

Tennis legend
Wimbledon champion

Tennis player Martina Navratilova holds the record for women's singles and doubles championships, with 167 and 163 titles, respectively. The dominant force in women's tennis for more than two decades, she won a record nine Wimbledon singles titles, six of which were earned consecutively from 1982 to 1987. Her achievement of 54 Grand Slam tournament titles (singles, doubles and mixed doubles) is second only to the record of Margaret Court Smith, who won 62.

GWILL LINDERME
YORK NEWMAN

*Civic activist and
Laurel School
Distinguished Alumna*

Through personal tragedy,
Gwill Linderme Newman
became deeply committed to
mental health advocacy and
served as the first woman president of the Brain Research
Foundation. She co-founded
the National Alliance for
Research on Schizophrenia
and Depression and PACT,
a nonprofit resource for families of the mentally disabled.
Newman also co-founded a
support group for the Playhouse Square Center theaters
in Cleveland, Ohio, served as
president of The Junior League
of Cleveland, Inc., and chaired
the Greater Cleveland Congress
of International Women's Year
in 1975. For her longtime civic
activism, Newman received the
Laurel School Distinguished
Alumna Award in 1989.

JOYCE
CAROL OATES

Novelist

One of the world's most pre-
eminent authors, Joyce Carol
Oates has been a prolific
writer since the age of 14.
Her acclaimed novels include
Bellefleur, *them*, *You Must Remember This*, *Solstice* and a
series of suspense novels published under the pseudonym
"Rosamond Smith." Oates
teaches in Princeton University's creative writing program
and, along with her husband,
operates a small press and
publishes a literary magazine,
The Ontario Review.

SANDRA DAY
O'CONNOR

U.S. Supreme Court Justice

Sandra Day O'Connor was the
first woman appointed to sit
on the U.S. Supreme Court.
Nominated to that position
by President Ronald Reagan
in 1981, O'Connor previously
sat on the Arizona Court of
Appeals and the Maricopa
County (Arizona) Superior
Court. After earning her law
degree at Stanford University
and starting a private practice,
she began her public career
as assistant attorney general
of Arizona. In 1969, she was
appointed to a vacant seat in
the Arizona state senate and
subsequently won reelection,
becoming senate majority
leader. She was the first woman
to hold that position.

MARY
PIPHER, PH.D.

*Clinical psychologist
and author*

Mary Pipher is a clinical
psychologist with a private
practice and is a visiting
professor at the University of
Nebraska. She is the author
of the bestsellers, *Reviving
Ophelia: Saving the Selves of
Adolescent Girls* and *The Shelter
of Each Other: Rebuilding Our
Families*, as well as *Hunger
Pains* and *Another Country*.
Additionally, Pipher is a commentator for Nebraska Public
Radio and a popular speaker
and workshop leader.

EUNICE
PODIS

Concert pianist

SALLY J.
PRIESAND

Rabbi

ROBERTA
COOPER RAMO

*Past president,
American Bar Association*

JANET
RENO

U.S. Attorney General

A widely acclaimed pianist, Eunice Podis has been a soloist with The Cleveland Orchestra nearly 100 times – a record-breaking number of engagements. Podis' concert career has spanned four decades and has taken her to many parts of the United States and Europe. Since 1966, she has served on the faculty of The Cleveland Institute of Music, and she has recorded solo and chamber works on the Telarc label.

Ordained in 1972 by Hebrew Union College-Jewish Institute of Religion in Cincinnati, Ohio, Sally J. Priesand became America's first woman rabbi. The Cleveland native has served synagogues in New York and New Jersey. She is the author of *Judaism and the New Woman* and is a contributor to *Women Rabbis: Exploration and Celebration*. The recipient of numerous awards and honors, Rabbi Priesand was named a Woman of Achievement by the Monmouth County (New Jersey) Advisory Commission on the Status of Women.

President in 1995-96 of the American Bar Association, the world's largest organization of attorneys, Roberta Cooper Ramo was the first woman to head the ABA. Ramo is a corporate law specialist with New Mexico's largest law firm and is a nationally sought-after speaker. Recipient of the Governor of New Mexico's Distinguished Public Service Award in 1993, she has served as president of the University of New Mexico Board of Regents and chair of the New Mexico Symphony Orchestra Board of Trustees. President Clinton appointed her to serve on the National Advisory Council on Violence Against Women.

Janet Reno, the nation's 78th Attorney General, is the first woman to hold that office. Prior to her 1993 appointment by President Clinton, Reno served for 15 years as Florida state attorney of Dade County, which has jurisdiction over the Greater Miami area. In this capacity, she managed an annual budget of $30 million and a yearly docket of 120,000 cases. Reno's previous legal experience includes serving as staff director of the Judiciary Committee of the Florida House of Representatives, as counsel for the state senate's committee responsible for revising the Florida criminal code and as a partner in a private Miami law firm.

LOUISE
RUSSERT-KRAEMER

Zoologist

DIANE
SAWYER

Broadcast journalist,
ABC News

PHYLLIS
SCHLAFLY

President, Eagle Forum

DONNA E.
SHALALA

U.S. Secretary of Health
and Human Services

Professor emerita of biological sciences at the University of Arkansas, Louise Russert-Kraemer is a nationally recognized expert on the biology and behavior of bivalved mollusks. She is a fellow of the American Association for the Advancement of Science, an editorial board member of *The Zoologist* and past president of the American Malacological Union and the American Microscopical Society. In addition to publishing numerous papers in technical fields of malacology (the study of mollusks), Russert-Kraemer has been a visiting fellow at Cambridge University.

Diane Sawyer joined ABC News in 1989 as co-anchor of "PrimeTime Live;" she is now a correspondent for "20/20." Previously, Sawyer spent nine years at CBS News as co-anchor of "60 Minutes" and of "CBS Morning News." Her extensive interviews and investigative reports have earned Emmy awards, an Alfred I. duPont-Columbia University Award and a George Foster Peabody Award for public service. Sawyer has also received a Lifetime Achievement Award from the Investigative Reporters and Editors Association.

Phyllis Schlafly has been a national leader of the conservative movement since the publication of her best-selling 1964 book, *A Choice Not An Echo*, and has been at the helm of the pro-family movement since 1972, when she started her national volunteer organization, Eagle Forum. Schlafly spreads her message widely, having authored or edited 16 books, in addition to writing a monthly newsletter, *The Phyllis Schlafly Report*, a syndicated column and regular radio commentaries. A lawyer, Schlafly has served as a member of the Commission on the Bicentennial of the U.S. Constitution and has testified before more than 50 congressional and state legislative committees on constitutional, national defense and family issues.

As Secretary of Health and Human Services, Donna Shalala is responsible for most of the nation's investments in health, basic science and welfare, comprising approximately 40 percent of the U.S. budget. Before joining the Clinton administration, Shalala was chancellor of the University of Wisconsin-Madison, the nation's largest public research university. Prior to that, she was president of Hunter College in New York. She is a native of Cleveland, Ohio.

CAROL
SHIELDS

*Pulitzer Prize-winning
author and educator*

Carol Shields is a professor
of English at the University of
Manitoba and chancellor of
the University of Winnipeg. A
novelist and playwright, she is
the author of *The Stone Diaries*,
Small Ceremonies, *The Box Garden*
and *Larry's Party*. Shields has
won numerous literary awards,
and was honored with the
Pulitzer Prize in 1995.

MURIEL
SIEBERT

*President and chairman,
Muriel Siebert and Company*

In 1967, Muriel Siebert became
the first woman to join 1,365
men in owning a seat on the
New York Stock Exchange. She
began her career in finance as
an associate in various brokerage firms. In 1967, she established Muriel Siebert and
Company, the nation's first
discount brokerage. Two
years later, Siebert became the
first woman superintendent of
banking for the State of New
York and then returned to her
own company, where she has
been chairman and president
since 1983.

RUTH J.
SIMMONS, PH.D.

President, Smith College

Ruth Simmons assumed the
presidency of Smith College
in 1995, becoming the first
African-American woman to
head a top-ranked institution of
higher education in the United
States. Former vice provost at
Princeton University and
provost at Spelman College,
she has taught at numerous
prestigious universities, has
served as an administrator at
the University of Southern
California and California State
University, and has authored
a book on education in Haiti.
In 1996, Dr. Simmons was
named CBS Woman of the
Year, NBC "Nightly News"
Most Inspiring Woman and
Glamour Magazine Woman
of the Year.

GLORIA
STEINEM

*Women's rights activist
and author*

Gloria Steinem is a consulting
editor for *Ms. Magazine*, the
international, feminist magazine
that she co-founded in 1972.
She is also the author of *Moving
Beyond Words*, a collection of
essays, and the best-selling
*Revolution from Within: A Book
of Self-Esteem*. Steinem is the
founding and current president of the Ms. Foundation
for Women and president
of Voters for Choice. She
has helped to establish the
Women's Action Alliance, the
National Women's Political
Caucus and the Coalition of
Labor Union Women.

NADINE
STROSSEN

*President, American Civil
Liberties Union*

Nadine Strossen, professor of
law at New York Law School,
has written, lectured and
practiced extensively in the
areas of constitutional law, civil
liberties and international
human rights. In 1991, she was
elected president of the American Civil Liberties Union and
was the first woman to serve
in that position. Strossen's
writings have been published
in numerous law reviews, magazines and newspapers; and her
book, *Defending Pornography:
Free Speech, Sex, and the Fight
for Women's Rights*, was named
a *New York Times* Notable Book
of 1995.

NINA
TOTENBERG

*Correspondent and commen-
tator, National Public Radio*

Nina Totenberg, National Public
Radio's legal affairs correspondent, is a regular commentator
on NPR's critically acclaimed
news magazines, "All Things
Considered," "Morning Edition" and "Weekend Edition."
Totenberg's coverage of the
Supreme Court and legal affairs
has won her widespread
recognition, and her ground-
breaking report about law professor Anita Hill's allegations
of sexual harassment by Judge
Clarence Thomas earned NPR
the prestigious Peabody Award.
A frequent contributor to major
newspapers and periodicals,
she has published articles in
The New York Times Magazine,
The Harvard Law Review, *The
Christian Science Monitor*, *Parade
Magazine* and others.

PATRICIA
M. WALD

*Circuit Judge,
U.S. Court of Appeals*

Judge Patricia Wald was
appointed U.S. Circuit Judge
for the District of Columbia
in 1979 and served as its chief
justice from 1986 to 1991.
Prior to her appointment to
the bench, Judge Wald was
assistant attorney general for
legislative affairs in the U.S.
Department of Justice and
an attorney for the Mental
Health Law Project. She is
a council member and first
vice president of the American
Law Institute and a fellow
of the American Academy of
Arts and Sciences.

FARAH M.
WALTERS

*President and chief executive
officer, University Hospitals
of Cleveland*

As president and chief executive
officer of University Hospitals
Health System and University
Hospitals of Cleveland, Farah
Walters presides over a healthcare network that includes more
than 10,000 physicians and
employees who serve patients
at more than 60 locations.
Walters has a 27-year background in health care and
health management and has
consulted and lectured for
major health organizations, such
as the Pan American Health
Organization, American Hosp-
ital Association and the U.S.
Army. In 1993, she was
appointed to Hillary Rodham
Clinton's National Health
Care Reform Task Force, and
that same year was selected by
Modern Healthcare as one of
the 50 individuals who are
shaping the future of health
care in America.

WENDY
WASSERSTEIN

*Pulitzer Prize-winning
playwright*

Wendy Wasserstein won the
Pulitzer Prize in drama and
a Tony Award for her 1988
play, *The Heidi Chronicles*.
Known for her Broadway hits
devoted to women and their
relationships, she has also
authored *The Sisters Rosensweig*
and *An American Daughter*.
Wasserstein co-authored the
screenplay, *The Object of My
Affection*, and her books include
Bachelor Girls, a collection of
essays, and *Pamela's First Musical*,
a children's book.

SARAH
WEDDINGTON

Plaintiff's attorney,
Roe v. Wade

A well-known spokesperson on
leadership and public issues,
Sarah Weddington was assistant
to President Jimmy Carter and
is now a writer, lecturer and
professor at the University
of Texas. Her first book, *A
Question of Choice*, detailed her
experiences with *Roe v. Wade*,
the case that gave women the
right to have an abortion, which
she successfully argued before
the U.S. Supreme Court in
1973. In 1972, Weddington
became the first woman from
Austin to be elected a member of the Texas House of
Representatives.

CHRISTINE TODD
WHITMAN

Governor of New Jersey

New Jersey's 50th chief executive, Christine Todd Whitman
is the state's first woman
governor. She is also the first
governor to give the formal
response to a President's State
of the Union Address. Whitman
is a former president of the
New Jersey Board of Public
Utilities and a former director
of the Somerset County (New
Jersey) Board of Freeholders.

index

STUDENT ARTWORK

a special thank you to all who made this book possible

Bye!